Dr. Ann Redding & Ann Campbell

To Kate
Blessings to you
and your K9 pals!

Ann Redding
Nov 08

TAILS *from* BEYOND

True Stories of Our Immortal Pets

Outskirts Press, Inc.
Denver, Colorado

Contents

The Authors

Remarkable Dogs Return From Beyond To Contact Their Families

A Horse Comes Back From The Other Side

Extraordinary Cats Send Afterlife Messages To Their Owners

Animals In Heaven

Evolution *of* Ann

I t is not my habit to let strangers into my house, but somehow this woman seemed different. It was October 2000. She was selling something – books, I think. She was stout, with gray hair, and appeared to be in her late fifties. We sat on my couch talking for a while until a lull in our conversation prompted the woman to look at me rather intently and tell me, "You're going to write a book."

I was surprised by her comment and quickly replied, "No, I'm not. I'm not a writer."

But the lady insisted, repeating, "Yes, you are going to write a book."

I responded with, "No, really. I have no intention of writing a book!" Once again, there was a pause in our conversation.

"Dear," the woman continued with a lingering stare, "you don't know this about me, but I'm psychic. You are definitely going to write a book." By then I was annoyed and decided that it was time for this stranger to leave. I continued to protest as I ushered her to the door.

As life sometimes goes, this messenger had the proverbial last laugh. Over time, various forces brought me to a pivotal point, at which I found myself compiling a book – a book I never intended to write! Even more amazing, the book was about the soul and existence in the afterlife, subjects I had not believed in for most of my life. Let me share with you how my point of view was changed, and what compelled me to write this book.

BORN A BIOLOGIST

Without hesitation, I can say that I was born a biologist. From the beginning I preferred fuzzy animals to dolls, and animals to people. My parents lovingly dubbed my bedroom "fungus corner," and that term suited me just fine. My bedroom was a sanctuary for numerous leaky aquariums filled with tadpoles and an assortment of fish. I also had several terrariums that housed turtles and frogs, as well as numerous coffee cans brimming with vegetation and various types of caterpillars. I spent hours taking care of these creatures and observing their behavior with great curiosity. Watching a butterfly emerge from its chrysalis became a favorite pastime. This intriguing event usually occurred around dinnertime, much to the irritation of my family. While everyone else was having dinner, I was engrossed in watching the birth of a new butterfly. I think my obsession with the animals disturbed my mother in particular, who hoped that I might become a model because I was tall and slender. The world of fashion glitz, coiffed hairdos, and layers of makeup held absolutely no appeal for me. Living amidst my animals eclipsed anything the outside world could possibly offer.

For my tenth birthday, my parents bought me my first dog. He was a brown Miniature Poodle and I proudly named him Coco, not realizing that practically everyone who has a brown Poodle calls it that. During my childhood, Coco was my best friend, my shadow, tagging along with me as I played with neighborhood friends.

At age 18, I headed off to college in Oregon, leaving Coco, my family, and the sunny weather of Southern California behind. It was a difficult adjustment for me, especially for the first two years, since the rainy weather prevented me from playing tennis and enjoying the other outside activities I loved so much. I was homesick and I missed my dog. In the third year, I took a class in general biology, and loving the subject, I was able to plunge myself deep into my studies. I was still eager, however, to return home each summer.

When I was 21, my life took a sudden turn. I became involved in a serious romantic relationship that did not meet the approval of my parents, who felt that my boyfriend was "not good enough" for me. Our conflict escalated as they attempted to keep me away from my love. After a few months, I ran away from home to get married in Oregon. The day I left, Coco was huddling beneath a coffee table, watching me intently. To this day, that memory of him haunts me. It was the last time I would see him. My family was so angry, they abandoned me and legally disowned me. The sting was devastating. No communication was permitted ... and my Christmas gifts were always returned.

I graduated from the University of Oregon in 1963 and my husband and I moved to Colorado, where I worked as a medical technologist. This proved to be the most difficult period in my life. I felt so alone, so far from home, so isolated from my family, and although I knew my parents would take care of Coco, I really missed seeing him. After a time, my husband and I decided to go to graduate school at the University of Colorado in Boulder. I wanted to study biology. Two years into my graduate studies, I was reunited with my parents, but my happy reunion was tainted by the sad news that Coco was dead. At the age of 16, he had been hit and killed by a car.

THE SCIENTIST

Graduate school thrilled me, and studying the subject I loved helped me to excel academically. For my doctoral thesis, I researched behavior and communication in five species of voles, small hamster-like rodents that burrow in the ground. I trapped them, bred them, and analyzed the high-frequency calls (ultrasounds) their babies produce during the first ten days of life. Because people can't hear these ultrasounds, virtually nothing was known about the pups' cries prior to my research. My husband helped me carry the voles in large, covered washtubs to the physics department, where a technician named Wolfgang used an ultrasonic detector to convert the high frequencies into audible sounds. A high-speed tape recorder picked up the ultrasounds on two-foot-wide spools, and played them back at a lower speed, which allowed the sounds to be analyzed by a spectrogram. I discovered that the structure of the ultrasounds was simple, possessing few harmonics. This simplicity, as well as the high frequency of the sounds, makes it difficult for predators to locate the nest. In all five species of voles the ultrasounds were identical, signifying that the calls were highly adaptive and effectively served to protect the babies. The baby rodents used these ultrasounds to communicate distress or danger, and both parents (especially the mother) ran quickly to a pup who was crying. Wolfgang often muttered in German, suggesting that I ought to be at home baking cookies for many small children. Later when my efforts were well received and my thesis was published, he finally managed to say something nice and congratulate me. After I earned my Ph.D. in 1970, my husband and I moved to California, where I taught biology and pre-nursing courses at Ventura College. Several years later, we were divorced.

Years of studying and teaching biology influenced me to think as a scientist with a materialistic and rational view of the world. I completely distrusted what could not be proved by traditional scientific method. I viewed the paranormal – mediums, out-of-body experiences, visions, past-life regression, and telepathy – as amusing figments of imagination. Believing in a soul and a life after death seemed mere wishful thinking by people who were afraid to face the truth. The truth, in my opinion, was that death led to oblivion, with no existence afterward. To be quite honest, during this time I felt superior to the "spiritual weaklings," who needed religious beliefs and faith to cope with the challenges of life.

STEPPING INTO THE MYSTICAL

I had taught for about 15 years when the first of three things happened that began to erode my scientific view of the universe. The first occurred one summer afternoon, as I was relaxing by a swimming pool. I suddenly felt paralyzed. Moments later I sensed that I was rising up and out of my body. For a few seconds I was conscious of hovering ten to fifteen feet in the air! I remember looking down from that position and seeing myself, lying on my back by the pool. I panicked! "What is happening?" I wondered. "If I drift any further from my body I will be dead!" Within seconds of thinking these thoughts, I re-entered my body. Afterward I kept asking

myself, "How could this have happened? How could I see myself without using my eyes? Are consciousness and awareness separate from the brain?"

A second event further challenged my logical mind-set. This time it came in the form of a powerful, mystical dream, which even now, almost 20 years later, remains vividly clear. On April 30, 1987, I dreamed that I was walking in the evening beside a large lake. The shore was brightly illuminated by a full moon, and the placid lake reflected the moonlight. The sound of honking geese caught my attention, and I looked up to the sky and saw a flock flying in a "V" formation. I continued walking and watching the geese as they flew ahead of me. At some point, my attention shifted from them to a white object in the sky, flying toward me. As it drew nearer, my mouth opened in amazement. "How can this be," I wondered. "It's Pegasus!" The mythical beast landed a short distance away and walked toward me until he stood so close that I could touch him. I could see the feathers on his wings and the individual hairs of his coat. He was larger than an ordinary horse, very muscular,

with dark eyes and a long mane and tail. His white coat seemed to radiate a heavenly glow. All I could do was stand motionless and gaze at him in awe. "How wonderful it would be to ride such a horse," I thought, but I wouldn't have dared to try because I was so overwhelmed by his presence. Too soon he backed away and reared up on his hind legs, towering above me! Then Pegasus turned away from me and galloped along the shoreline. Gradually his image grew smaller, until eventually he spread his wings and ascended into the sky. Mesmerized by the experience, I watched him disappear from view.

Suddenly, I was awake. My awareness shifted from the dream to my bedroom, and for many minutes, I was disoriented and confused as to which was real. I thought my bedroom must be the dream! It was extremely difficult to accept that my encounter with Pegasus had not been real. I wondered why this dream had been so vivid. If it was just a dream, how could it feel just as real as anything I had ever experienced? Why did I have this dream? What did it mean?

I took a class in dream analysis to help find the answers. From the class, I became open to the possibility that somehow during sleep my consciousness had shifted and had allowed me to enter the astral world, where some believe that Pegasus actually exists. Another interpretation involved Pegasus as a symbol of my "higher" self, beckoning me to a more spiritual level of consciousness. In any case, searching for answers was pushing me away from the scientific world to the realm of the paranormal. I began to read books on metaphysics. My mind was opening to the possibility that we live in a multi-dimensional universe, which we can know and experience if we move beyond our physical senses and rational thinking. After all, even science acknowledges that human eyes, ears, and other receptors can process only a tiny amount of the total energy that surrounds us.

SEEKING THE SOUL

Six years after my dream of Pegasus, I received an afterlife communication from my father. We had shared a close relationship when I was younger, spending happy hours at the beach, hiking in the mountains, fishing, ice-skating, and playing tennis or Ping-Pong. Because my dad was a medical doctor and scientifically oriented, we often discussed current ideas about medicine and evolution, as well as the origin and nature of the universe. My dad was a religious person, and he frequently expressed his spiritual views. He was a staunch believer in the existence of the soul and eternal life. In contrast, I thought that there was no such thing as the soul, and that both existence and consciousness ended at death. As you can imagine, this clash of ideas led to some interesting and heated debates.

In August 1993, my 83-year-old father was hospitalized with cancer. I went to San Diego to see him, and to be with my mother, who was having a hard time coping with his illness. As I entered the hospital room, Dad opened his eyes very wide and looked at me for a long time. Although he did not say it, I knew he was telling me that he was happy that I had come, and that he knew I would help my mother. Mom and I talked to him for about an hour, until she left to do some errands. I remained with my father, who by then had fallen asleep. When Mother returned, we considered spending the night at the hospital, but we left when the nurse encouraged us to go home and get some rest and come back in the morning. At 11:00 o'clock, we had a call from the hospital to tell us that Dad had died. We were shocked! Just a few hours earlier we had been talking to him, and Dad had even walked around the room by himself. I sobbed uncontrollably after hearing the news, and throughout the funeral a few days after his death. My sadness was profound. I had lost a parent and a dear friend.

After the funeral, I tried to resume my normal schedule. Training my dogs was always pleasurable, so I decided to take my Poodles to the park for some relaxation. I set up a ring with jumps and spent several hours happily training and playing with my canine companions. It was a wonderful, if only temporary, relief from my sadness! Feeling quite cheerful and relaxed, I started to leave the park to join my mother and my sister Jane for lunch.

As I opened the van door, I suddenly felt an energy or "presence" around me. Within seconds I heard a masculine voice exclaim, "The soul is energy!" The message was distinct and delivered in a bold, confident, matter-of-fact style. Without a doubt, I knew this was not my own thought but a message from my father. From eternity, he had reached out to tell me what I needed to hear. It changed my view of the universe instantly. I realized that my dad still existed, and that indeed there was an afterlife. I knew there really was a soul, and that it was a form of energy, not a tangible object as I had always imagined. "Why hadn't I ever thought of that before?" I wondered. Feelings of gratitude swept over me as my eyes filled with tears. My father's message had transformed me and had given me a glimpse of eternity – the ultimate gift of love. Over and over I kept saying, "Oh, my God . . . Oh, my God." Then as I looked around, I was startled to see that the park was turning from green to gold. The last piece of equipment I was carrying slipped from my hand as an unearthly light illuminated the park in every direction. I moved away from the van, completely overwhelmed by what I was seeing. The leaves on the trees appeared like yellow coins, with the sun's rays enhancing their brilliant hue. I remember standing under one of the large trees, watching the glistening leaves move rhythmically with the gentle breeze. Time seemed to stand still. Nothing existed but a vague sense of self and the brilliant gold tones surrounding me. I felt so humble, so grateful, so blissful, so loved. Many minutes passed – I know, because I recall walking several times in a large circle, observing this wonderland.

Eventually the dazzling colors began to fade and the green tones of nature returned. I drove home, still in a daze, thinking about what had happened. When I told my mother, she reacted with skepticism and told me that I had an overactive imagination. My sister believed me, though! She told me excitedly that the previous night, she had awakened to a beautiful, unearthly, golden light. As she sat up in bed, a profound sense of love and peace came over her, which she recognized instinctively as coming from our dad. When she put her head back on the pillow, the intense sensations began to sweep over her again, and she heard the message, "Pay attention!" Apparently Dad wanted to be certain that Jane understood him: he existed, he was doing fine, and he loved her very much.

WRITING A BOOK

Four years after my father died, I retired from teaching biology at Ventura College. By that time, I had taught for 27 years, and decided to leave in order to devote more time to training and enjoying my dogs. I bought a lovely home with a big backyard so that I could set up agility equipment to train and play with my dogs.

In November 2002, one of my dogs, Tasha, died, and surprised me by returning to visit in a vivid dream. Just three months later, my Poodle Rudy died unexpectedly. He returned several times to console me as I coped with debilitating grief. Although several of my pets had died previously, I had never experienced afterlife contacts with them. The "visits" from Tasha and Rudy inspired me to read about afterlife communication with pets, but to my surprise, I found few publications devoted specifically to animals. As I talked to my friends, I learned that some of them had enjoyed similar experiences, but had been reluctant to share their stories. My encounters with Tasha and Rudy were so meaningful, mysterious, and powerful, I felt compelled to discover more about pets and the afterlife. Almost without realizing what was happening, I began to collect stories from other pet owners, and before I knew it, I was writing a book, just as the stranger had predicted!

There are 47 stories in *Tails from Beyond*, all voluntarily submitted. I am pleased that so many people trusted me enough to share these intimate stories! To obtain information from the owners, I used e-mails, questionnaires, and conversations. I usually communicated with each person several times before feeling satisfied that I had enough information, and that the story was valid. I sent contributors a working draft of their story and had them sign to verify the accuracy, and to give me permission to publish. Minor descriptions were sometimes added later to enhance the stories, but the details of the paranormal experiences were never altered.

Many people were involved in the production of this book. In the beginning, I worked with Zee Designs and they did a wonderful job copying the photographs I sent them. I also worked with Ann Castro, a lovely lady and professional writer, who helped me compose the stories. Two years into the project, I found another person to help me with the writing – Ann Campbell. We shared a name and a fascination with the stories, and her contribution to my project became so important, I thought it was only right to make her co-author. I was the person who gathered the facts and wrote the essentials. The other Ann was the storyteller who added richness and color and made the stories come alive. I feel so grateful to have found this charming lady, who gave so much of herself to this project and who has become a cherished friend. I was also lucky to have Laura Uran as one of my artists. Whenever adequate photos were not available, Laura would sketch the animals in black and white. In every case the owners were delighted and commented that the drawings were true to the appearance of their animals. Both Laura and Ann contributed personal stories of their afterlife encounters with their pets. Laura Young, my author representative at Outskirts Press, helped me through the final stages of publication. Bill Knott sketched ten original colored illustrations for the book and Lewis Agrell created the colored borders and a collage, which serves as a background for the Table of Contents and last page in the book. Sonya D. Woods worked on the photographs, making sure they were clear enough to print. Victoria Wood somehow managed to successfully photograph me with my five poodles! My mother and sister Jane were always there to encourage me, as were three friends, Donna Warsoff, Barb Kraatz, and Tom Holstein. My friend, Flavia Potenza was kind enough to read all the stories and give me her suggestions. Last and definitely not least, I am grateful that my friend Dawn Reed used her talents and artistic skills to create my website *www.TailsfromBeyond*.

The one common denominator for all of these afterlife encounters was a strong, intimate, loving bond between the person and the animal. I discovered that pets usually contacted owners because there were unresolved issues or because owners were having extreme difficulty coping with the loss of their pet. However, the ultimate answer as to why some pets return while others do not still remains a mystery to me.

Creating this book helped me overcome the intense grief I felt after losing my two poodles. The book gave me a chance to honor my dogs who had returned to console me after their death and I was happy to give other people the same opportunity to share their stories. As I wrote about others' experiences, I became more convinced of the validity of my own encounters. Over and over again, I heard stories that seemed to confirm the existence of life after death. My life took on new meaning as I created the book. It moved me beyond the routine, mundane and selfish pursuits of self-gratification. The project gave my life a new purpose, a spiritual mission to spread the good news that indeed there is an afterlife for our beloved pets. The book became a gift of hope and consolation that would endure beyond my lifetime.

May these true stories illuminate, inspire and give you peace, as they have done for me.

…Dr. Ann Redding

The Other Ann

My obsession with animals began rather late in life, although I had a lot of rabbits and a nomadic Irish Water Spaniel named Cunningham when I was growing up. I have a favorite Cunningham story, which I may try to sneak into this book, even though Cunningham didn't come back. He is probably still wandering around on the Other Side, looking for an exit!

I am a retired teacher of English, literature and writing in particular, and was supervisor of yearbook production at South High School in Denver for more than 20 years. Do not, however, imagine me with sturdy shoes and a gray bun at the back of my head. My uniform is a sweatshirt and jeans in the winter, and a T-shirt and shorts in summer. My hair hasn't been long enough in years to make anything like a bun, and I'm almost always barefoot.

It was the idea of several friends that I needed a dog that summer of 1967. My father died during my first summer vacation in Denver. During the second summer, I was privileged to attend the University of Edinburgh to study 18th century history and literature. The English-Speaking Union sent me there on a scholarship, and it was wonderful to return to the country of my ancestors. I had the opportunity to travel around the lowlands and the highlands and learn just how upset some people still were over the fact that the Campbells had enjoyed the hospitality of the MacDonalds in Glencoe in 1692, and then had murdered them in their beds. If you want all the facts, you can look up the Battle of Glencoe on the Internet. As that third summer approached, I had nothing in particular to look forward to. My roommate flew off to Delaware to be married. I had already visited my sister and her family in Utah.

I was not looking for a dog. I had seen and admired my friend's lovely and obedient Sheltie, and then she had seven puppies just a few days after my birthday. After six were born, Jo had cleaned everything up and put mother and babies to bed, but some time in the night, my little Robbie sneaked in — or out — or both. Then everyone started. "You've got to get a puppy!" Of course I had birthday money from my brother, Bob, and I could not resist that tiny black, white, and tan baby who snuggled into my hand, and that led to my getting a house, and then another Sheltie and another, until there were at least a dozen and I was hooked on breeding, training, and showing dogs, and was very active in our Colorado Sheltie club.

I became the editor of our monthly newsletter in September of 1978 and kept the job for 25 years. During that time I also produced the complete 1988 American Shetland Sheepdog Association's *Handbook*, and did a lot of writing, rewriting, and editing on another Sheltie publication. It was while I was editing *The Colorado Sheltie* that I was introduced to Dr. Ann Redding's plan for this book. I corrected my own story when it was sent to me, and was then invited to check the rest of the stories for grammar and spelling. That led to a surprising lot of writing, rewriting, and editing, and before I knew it, I was the "co-author" of the book! I became Ann Redding's "curator of migratory words."

Although I have been a Coloradoan for more than 40 years, I still feel like the South Dakota native I am. I was born on the edge of the Rosebud Indian Reservation, in Dallas, SD, the youngest of five children, and grew up in Sioux Falls. I graduated from the University of South Dakota, and after that I lived and either taught or studied in Michigan, England, Switzerland, and Kentucky. We still live in the house I bought in Denver in 1968, across the street from my school, and we still have two Shelties, but they are not shown or bred. We also have a very entertaining little brown Poodle, all seven or eight pounds of him, who bosses those girl dogs and reminds them constantly that he is in charge.

My experience with life after death came from my first two Shelties, but it did not strike me forcefully until my closest brother, Dean, came to say goodbye to me shortly after his death on May 31, 1995. I was alone in the house, writing checks at my desk. There was no dryer sheet or perfume ad or any other source of the sweet odor that engulfed me about five o'clock. I looked everywhere, sniffing the air, but the heavenly scent, which was all around me, did not originate in this house. When my niece called to let me know that Dean had died after long suffering and disability from malignant melanoma, which had metastasized to his brain and other organs, she set the time of death at 6 p.m. in Memphis, 5 p.m. in Denver. I knew then that Dean had come to say goodbye and had surrounded me with "the odor of sanctity."

Here are the stories of some beloved pets who returned with the message, "I am well. I am whole. I am happy, and I will always love you." I have no idea how it happens, or why so few come back, even briefly, to let us know that our profession of belief in "the life everlasting" is not a mere sequence of words. It is our Creed, and it is true, in the depths of our minds and hearts and very being.

...Ann Campbell

Dogs

"If I should go before you, do not weep. I shall be chasing butterflies

in the fields that never die. There will be rabbits and chipmunks

and I shall run in the sweet air. The Master will smile at me,

because He smiled when I was made and all my kind. I shall play

while the stars wheel about me, then come to the gate to wait for

you. For when you come, I shall be there, waiting to frolic at your heels

and give you love I have been saving. We shall walk together,

you and I, until the centuries are multi-colored ashes."

Ann B. Hoversen, Ph.D.
Used by Permission

Girl

...an energetic Lab-mix dog who won the heart of Kathy Shafer, a southern Californian, and died a tragic death when she was just six years old. Kathy does non-anesthetic teeth cleaning for dogs and cats.

I was in my house one day when I heard a puppy barking. Stepping outside, I saw the "critter" who was responsible for the noise. A slender, black Lab-mix with long legs stood just outside the fence surrounding my front yard. I guessed she was three or four months old.

"What are you doing?" I asked. Seeing no one with her, I approached the pup. "Come on over here," I coaxed. She seemed eager to respond, even though there was a fence between us. Realizing she couldn't go through the fence, she wisely circled around it to get to me. "Now that's a smart dog," I thought, and since she wore no identification, I claimed her as mine.

Once I had her inside, I took a good look at her. She was petite with dainty facial features and golden eyes. As she had such a feminine appearance, I immediately thought of the name "Girl." This seemed appropriate, because I owned a young male Afghan called "Guy."

From the beginning, Girl and I felt a strong connection. She was, without a doubt, my special dog, and I took her with me as often as possible. When she was full grown, Girl weighed about 30 pounds. She was energetic and so remarkably agile, that I even taught her to go up a ladder and to climb trees! Never fearful of heights, she would climb as high as possible and go up into the branches. All it would take were a few words of encouragement from me, and up she'd go!

She loved to play games in the house and outside, and she was crazy about water. One of her favorite outdoor games, which we called "Water Fall," involved the garden hose. Often in the evening, I would turn the hose on and watch as Girl ran and jumped over and under and around the stream of water. Inside the house, our bathtub became the target for her games. We had one of those old-fashioned stoppers with a chain and Girl loved to jump into the tub and toss the stopper and chain against the porcelain sides. She would roll the stopper, nudge it, and throw it again and again, loving the noise and appearing to be fascinated by the commotion.

Besides being agile, playful, and smart, Girl was incredibly gentle, never wanting to harm anything intentionally. One night, I noticed she was carefully removing books from the lowest shelf of my bookcase. Methodically, she took out one book and then another. "What is going on?" I wondered. Suddenly I knew. Girl had found a mouse hiding behind the books, but she just wanted to play with it. She had no intention of killing her catch. In fact, Girl dropped the little creature as soon as I told her to put it down. She also liked to "go fishing" in our aquarium. Standing over the tank, Girl would plunge her nose into the water and grab a fish. When I told her to put the fish back into the water, she would release it unharmed.

One day I noticed that Girl was standing still in the backyard, holding her tail out straight while bending one front leg. She maintained the pointer's stance, looking down at the ground, never moving a muscle. Only her eyes moved, shifting back and forth as if beckoning me. Curious, I went to see what was going on. There, fluttering on the ground, was a sparrow entangled in a string. As I unraveled the string to free the bird, Girl waited quietly by my side. Then the two of us watched as the little sparrow flew away.

I usually took Girl with me when I went out, but one particular day, it was just too hot. Afraid she might get out of the yard since she was such a good climber and jumper, I secured her in our dog run with a lead attached to a pulley. Guy, my other dog, was also in the run, but not restrained. Knowing the two dogs had water and shade, I left for work, expecting to return late in the afternoon. That morning, around 10:30, I had a sudden premonition that Girl was in danger, but I was unable to leave work until noon. Then I drove 30 minutes to get home, all the while with a knot in my stomach and a terrible feeling that something was wrong.

My worst fears were realized when I ran to the backyard and found that Girl's lead was caught on a bolt protruding from the fence where the dog run was attached. She had been trapped in the scorching sun, unable to get to the water or the shade, and she was already suffering from heat stroke. She was still conscious and recognized me, smiling her bright smile as if to say, "I knew you would come." Immediately I wrapped her in cold towels to lower her body temperature, and filled the tub with cold water. I sat down in the tub, put Girl on my lap, and worked on her for several hours. For a long time, I simply held her in the water. When my husband came home from work at four o'clock, he drove us to the vet. On the way, I sensed my dog's soul leaving her body, and I had little hope that she would recover. A few hours later, the vet called me at home to tell us that Girl was dead. I didn't go back to retrieve her body. For me, it was just a shell that she had existed in. It wasn't Girl.

After Girl died, I was inconsolable. I wailed and cried; the intensity of my grief amazed me. It was so tremendously difficult losing her, but my feelings of guilt were even harder to bear. My mind flooded with thoughts of "If only" and "I should have." Finally, after a month of torturing myself, I felt my grief subside and knew that I needed to move on.

About six months after her death, I saw Girl again. It was a summer afternoon around five, and the sun was shining as I waited for my order outside a local taco restaurant. My car was parked about eight feet away. I turned from watching the cook and glanced toward my car, and there was Girl! She was sitting in the driver's

seat, waiting for me as she always had. Her tongue was hanging out and her golden eyes were sparkling. I was momentarily stunned and could not move. Although I didn't doubt what I was seeing, I wanted someone else to see her, too, to validate my vision. Without taking my eyes off Girl, I began to tap gently on the counter to get the cook's attention, but he did not respond. I tapped for about 15 seconds, and then my eyes began to burn as I stared at the apparition. When I finally blinked, Girl was gone. The driver's seat was empty.

I don't believe that Girl visited me for a particular reason. She had simply returned to something familiar, something that felt good to her. My dog was behaving as she always had, moving into the driver's seat whenever I left the car. And she probably is still doing that even today. The only difference is that on that particular day, I was able to see her.

Seeing Girl made my heart smile. For one brief moment, I was privileged to have confirmation of existence beyond death. I remember feeling so grateful for this gift, and saying, "Thank you! Thank you!" I tucked the experience into my spiritual "back pocket." It exists as a quiet knowing, kept safely within me.

Tasha

...a Toy Poodle who was cherished for almost 16 years in the home of her owner, Dr. Ann Redding. Tasha was the first to give this retired biology professor and dog trainer a glimpse of animals on the Other Side.

Tasha was born in my living room, and in all the excitement of toweling down the wiggly, wet babies and urging them to nurse, I thought she was black like her mother. But after the two puppies were dry and warm, I discovered that she was colored like rich, dark chocolate — and if you know Poodles, you know that the chocolate ones are the rascals of the breed. From the beginning, this pup was independent and feisty. She never played with her little brother or her mother, preferring instead to wander off to investigate the house and get into trouble. Trouble meant getting into the peat moss I had placed around the base of my numerous artificial plants and scattering it all over the house, making a mess everywhere! Trouble also meant attacking the knobs at the base of the toilets, which covered the screws securing the toilet to the floor. She would bark at them, pounce on them, and chew them until they came loose. Her favorite naughtiness, though, was beating up on her gentle little brother, who was such a sweet boy, always trying to be perfect in every way. Even as a puppy, it was nearly impossible for me to turn Tasha onto her back, which is a common exercise to establish the human being as the head of the pack. She fought tooth and nail every time I tried. When it came time for the puppy temperament test, she scored as high as possible for "dominance." I was thankful that she would not grow up to be an 80-pound Rottweiler!

When Tasha was mature, she was 11 inches tall at the shoulder, and weighed about eight pounds — just an inch too tall to be a Toy and far too small to be a "competitive" Miniature, but she was well-proportioned and a real beauty, with her thick, chocolate coat and fluffy "Dumbo" ears. Her eyes reminded me of the button eyes on teddy bears — brown and penetrating, daring to look right at me. She was a little sprite, energetic and always running through the grass searching for puffy dandelions. Once she found them, she pounced on them gleefully and caused the seeds to disperse everywhere. I am sure she was responsible for many little yellow flowers throughout southern California!

Tasha loved to chase a ball, so I bought her a small, blue rubber ball that I affectionately called "Boo." We spent hours playing with Boo. It was my custom, after our game, to pick up my little girl and ask her for a kiss. Without fail, she turned her head away and looked in the opposite direction. "Oh, come on. Just a little kiss," I pleaded, as I tapped her face to try and get her attention. But she would not look at me, preferring instead to stare into the distance at some imaginary and endlessly fascinating object! Of course she knew exactly what I wanted. If I persevered, she would eventually give me the world's briefest kiss and then resume her gaze into the distance as quickly as possible.

I'll never forget the day she discovered the power of her bark. A large dog approached us in the park, and I could tell she was intimidated, but she held her ground. When the dog was about ten inches from her, she suddenly barked right into his face. He backed away from her, and little Tasha had the "light bulb" experience. She barked again, and the bully backed away even more. At this point, she turned into Tasha the Tiger, barking and lunging at him until he turned and ran away. From that point on, things were never the same in our house. She barked whenever she wanted something, and she wanted it NOW. She had a loud bark and little patience! She scolded me if her dinner wasn't ready on time, or if I wasn't awake and up by 6:30! When one of her little tennis balls rolled under the couch, Tasha would run to me to announce her predicament. She stood very tall (11 inches can seem pretty tall!), looked directly into my eyes, and barked until I responded and retrieved the toy for her. As this began to occur with some regularity, it dawned on me that she was doing it on purpose! One evening I watched to confirm my hunch. Sure enough, I saw the little brat deliberately push the ball under the couch with her nose. Afterward, she began barking and ran to find me, her obedient servant, to pull the ball out for her!

When she was young, I began to train Tasha in obedience. Her love of food and toys made the process relatively easy. Competing, however, was a different matter. Being such a small dog, her heeling — walking and running along with me on my left side — was a bit erratic, especially if the surface was irregular or the grass was long. Her scent articles and dumbbell were so tiny they were often invisible in the long grass. One time in an outdoor ring, Tasha spent almost five minutes searching for the little dumbbell I had thrown. When she found it, she pounced on it with the utmost glee! Her pouncing reminded me of the way she acted when she found puffy dandelions. As she came running to bring the dumbbell to me, the crowd cheered and my heart soared.

Despite our difficulties and challenges, Tasha and I prevailed. She earned the prestigious OTCH title (Obedience

Trial Champion) on July 11, 1993. I was so proud, and fondly remember our demonstration that day. Before an applauding crowd, my little girl pranced happily along at my left side, looking up attentively, waiting for her treat. As always, she held her head up very high and watched me as we moved in synchrony. What joy I felt!

As Tasha aged, she became incontinent and had to wear diapers. She lost her hearing and then, even worse, her sight in both eyes. Hoping to enhance the quality of her life, I took her for cataract surgery when she was 15. The operation was successful. I remember when she saw me again for the first time after being blind for months. She blinked a few times and then really looked at me. Never has a moment been more precious to me. I hugged her and wept.

For about five wonderful months, Tasha was able to see. Then, almost without warning, she was blind again. Inflammation had caused her loss of vision, and this time there was damage to the retina, with no hope of recovery. The vet had never warned me about this potential complication so many months after the surgery. For weeks I felt extremely angry, sad, and frustrated. Even now I have residual feelings about this horrible turn of events. After losing her sight a second time, Tasha deteriorated quickly. Within a few months, she became feeble and thin. Realizing that her quality of life was poor and that she would never regain her health, I decided to euthanize her at home. The process was peaceful and quick.

Within four days of losing Tasha, I had a remarkably vivid dream. Shortly before I awoke, I saw my little girl running toward me. She had regained her spunky, vivacious nature. Her coat was thick, beautiful, and dark brown again. As she jumped on my chest, I felt the weight of her body. I sensed her warm, wet tongue giving me kisses all over my face, as she licked me with great exuberance. I reached to hug her and plunged my fingers into her dense brown coat, feeling her warmth and the texture of her hair. Sensations of joy and intimacy, of relief and exhilaration swept over me, and I began to weep. My "contact dream" lasted about 15 seconds before I awoke. Tears of joy streamed down my face, but soon my joy changed to desperation when I realized that Tasha was gone. I called her name several times, wanting so much to be with her again.

An ordinary dream is usually nonsensical, vague, and quickly forgotten, but when a dream is a contact from the Other Side, sensations are heightened so that a person is sure the event actually took place. A contact dream leaves a powerful impression, and details including feelings and messages are easily remembered. This dream remains as real as any conscious experience I have ever had. Tasha was truly there, and three years later, the details of the "dream" are still vivid in my memory. It was as though our souls met briefly on a different plane of existence. I believe Tasha contacted me to let me know she was fine and that euthanizing her had been the right and loving thing to do. Her visit let me know how much she loved me, and now that she was on the Other Side, she could finally drop the "attitude" and let me know by bathing my face with kisses!

Exactly one year to the day after her passing, I was startled to find in my backyard a small, blue rubber ball identical to "Boo." I had tucked Tasha's ball into a box of mementos and was sure it could not have gotten out without help! For the next few days, I discovered more blue balls in my backyard. It was some time before I learned that the balls came from the children who were playing next door. Even so, the timing of their appearance was extraordinary.

Tasha's ashes remain with me on an altar in my house, and they will join mine when I die. An area of my garage is "Tasha's Corner," where I display many of her ribbons and awards won in obedience. In my photo album are precious pictures taken while she was at home or competing in obedience. And how could I forget Tasha's bark? I recorded it on my answering machine and called it the "bark beep." Now Tasha's voice will always be with me and available for all to hear before they leave a message.

Sally Forth

...she was the sickest and the cutest pup at the shelter, and she stole the heart of Laura Uran. She will steal yours, too! Sally spent 14 short years with Laura, the daughter of Bernice Halsey, who has contributed her story of "Sam." Laura is one of the artists for this book and is also an RN, a counselor, and animal behavior consultant who spends her spare time hiking and painting.

Before I went to the pound to choose a dog, I told myself not to lose my heart to some sickly pup or runt. Then I saw Sally. She was thin, had diarrhea, and was fearful of people — and she was the last pup in the litter. Nevertheless, Sally was cute, and something about her caught my attention. I left, but came right back, knowing I couldn't resist her, and I have never regretted my decision.

Her diarrhea turned out to be inflammatory bowel disease, for which she was given large doses of prednisone. I didn't want to keep her on this medication too long, so I searched for weeks in the library to find alternative natural remedies. My hard work paid off, and I was able to stabilize her condition for most of her life with the use of herbs. A vet told me later that it was a miracle she lived for over 14 years. Most dogs with this disease are dead within three. Then that same vet smiled sweetly and said, "I think it's the love between you two that was responsible for her longevity."

Despite her illness, Sally enjoyed great quality of life. She was adventuresome, loved hiking, and enjoyed being involved in everything the family did. I trained her in obedience, which proved to be easy because she wanted so much to please me. Difficulties arose, however, when we were with other people because Sally was afraid of strangers and did not like to be left alone in an unfamiliar place. I had to be careful about leaving her on the long sit and long down exercises. It took some time to work through her fears, but once Sally understood that she was safe and that I was returning, she was no longer afraid and could remain in place consistently and enthusiastically.

I'm extremely proud of our accomplishments in obedience. One year, Sally was recognized by AMBOR (American Mixed Breed Obedience Registration) for having the highest Open level average in the nation. Another year, Sally attained the highest Utility average. In addition, she obtained the first 200 (perfect) score in obedience in the history of AMBOR, under an AKC judge. Sally also won the Hero Dog Award for driving off three men who tried to pull me into a car when we were out walking. When I needed help, my shy canine friend forgot about herself and turned into a ferocious attack dog!

My most satisfying achievement was training Sally to be a therapy dog. She had to interact with the elderly and sick people, as well as mentally challenged or abused children. One time a child who had not spoken in weeks began to tell Sally about her abusive past. Imagine, Sally, who had been so afraid of people, was connecting with others and relating to them in the most intimate and comforting way! It was uncanny how many people opened up to her. There was something special about Sally. You could see it in her eyes. She had the eyes of a wise soul, a being who understood suffering. Many people told me she seemed to be much more than just a dog. Indeed, she was.

I adored Sally, which made watching her grow more ill even more difficult. Eventually, it became apparent that her inflammatory bowel disease couldn't be controlled any longer, as she began to waste away. In addition, she had suffered from laryngeal paralysis when she was 13, and had surgery to assist her breathing. Knowing that Sally was in pain, I was forced to make the tough decision to have my special pal euthanized and cremated. Her passing overwhelmed me. I couldn't sleep and when I was awake I could hardly function because I was constantly crying. I felt a heavy weight around my heart, which was truly broken.

A few days after Sally's passing, I walked into the area where her bed had been. Suddenly, the beautiful fragrance of roses surrounded me. It was so noticeable that I could have sworn a rose was being held right under my nose. The scent was delicate and exquisite, but not at all overpowering. When I stepped away from the place where Sally had slept, the fragrance was absent, but if I returned to the area, it came back, and lasted several minutes. When I told others about this wonderful scent, they bombarded me with questions: Were the windows open? Were there flowers in the house? Was I using a scented dryer sheet? The answer to all their

inquiries was the same: " No!" Even if any of these things had been true, why was the scent only in the area of Sally's bed?

About a week later, I smelled the fragrance again. This time it came from under the kitchen table, one of Sally's favorite places to rest. For a while, the scent puzzled me until I realized that somehow, in this fragrance, Sally was visiting me! Once I understood, I felt relieved, honored, and joyful, because I knew that Sally was safe, faring well, and doing her best to comfort me. Some time later, I read that roses are the "scent of the soul," and recalled that roses are the flower associated with the Virgin Mary. This brought back a very special memory.

My husband and I had traveled to Sioux City, Iowa, to see a place called Trinity Heights, a beautiful wooded area covering 70 acres. There, standing atop a rise, is an awe-inspiring, 30-foot statue of Mary. Sally went with us, and when we got to the statue of Mary, she did the most amazing thing. She looked up toward the face of Mary and stared at it. After a bit, she wagged her tail, jumped up on the platform, and began to lick the toes of the statue! Then she lay down by the feet of Mary and placed her head on one foot! It was obvious that Sally wanted to stay there for a while, so we did not disturb her. The incident almost took our breath away. Some of the other visitors at the shrine saw what had happened and they had tears in their eyes. Once again, someone remarked that Sally was extraordinary and seemed almost human.

Sally's passing impacted all of us. My other dog Kes missed Sally and looked all over the house for her. A few days after the remarkable fragrance sweetened the area around Sally's bed, I was sitting in the living room with Kes. Out of the blue, Kes let out her "greeting" whine and grabbed a toy. With a canine grin and a wagging rear end, she play-bowed and darted around as she always did whenever she saw Sally. She licked a space close to me, which would have been at the height of Sally's face, and then began to whine again in excitement. It was obvious that she was looking at something. Suddenly Kes's mood changed. She turned to me with a puzzled expression, and began to glance all around as if she were confused. Apparently, whatever she had seen was no longer there. Her ears drooped and she came back to sit with me. I believe that Sally visited Kes to say goodbye, and to explain where she had gone. Afterward, Kes perked up and became more playful, and stopped looking for her old pal.

Although my grief lessened in some ways, it continued in others. Sometimes when I awoke, I would reach for Sally in my bed, only to realize that she was gone.

One evening a stray cat came into our yard and I couldn't get him to leave. The cat insisted on sitting by my feet or by my husband. He wouldn't budge from the position, even if Kes threatened him. The cat acted as though he belonged to us. Some time in the night, I woke up crying, and got out of bed so I wouldn't disturb my husband. I heard a scratching at the patio door, and there was the cat! I put on a coat and took food and water to him. He gulped down the food, just as Sally always had. Afterward, he jumped into my lap and pressed against my body, exactly the way Sally used to do. I held the cat for a while, and felt very tired but no longer sad. Then I put him down and went back to bed, where I slept peacefully for a change.

The next morning the cat was there again, and again, I fed him. He gulped down the food as he had done before, and then the two of us wandered into the woods behind our house. I loved sitting there and enjoying the quiet. As I sat, the cat came and pressed himself against me. For two hours this little animal stayed with me, touching me and looking into my eyes — just as Sally used to do. I hugged him, cried, and talked to him. His presence soothed and comforted me. It was as if Sally were there in the body of this cat!

Eventually, my grief began to subside. When it did, the cat disappeared, but he would invariably show up at the door whenever I started to feel depressed and grief-stricken again. His appearance and disappearance according to my mood was uncanny! I would have kept my new feline friend, but I had a bird and wasn't comfortable having a strange cat in the house with us. I wanted to find a special home for him, and decided to call my friend, who had just lost her kitty. The timing was perfect, and she agreed to take him. As I began to describe the cat to her, my friend stopped me. "Laura," she said, "does that description remind you of anyone?" I was shocked to realize that several of the cat's physical features were similar to Sally's. Was it grief that kept me from noticing it before?

On the cat's black face was a marking that created the illusion of a large white, handlebar moustache, exactly where Sally had a moustache that fluffed out on both sides of her mouth. There was a small, perfectly square, hairless area on Sally's neck left by the throat surgery. The stray cat had a square white patch, exactly the same size and in precisely the same spot as Sally's scar. The similarities between the cat and Sally flabbergasted me, especially because it is so unusual to find perfectly precise, square markings of contrasting color in an animal's fur.

Since childhood, I have believed that animals have souls, and that they live on after death. Even a priest couldn't convince me otherwise, despite his bullying me and reporting my "heresy" to my mother, who believed as I did! Since then, I have found support for my convictions in my afterlife experiences with Sally, and in several biblical references. I was so fortunate that Sally became a part of my life. She was truly a Guru wrapped in a dog's coat. Now as I look at her shiny trophies and awards, I realize they honor her, but that they can't compare with the glorious light in her eyes.

Lindsey

...a tiny, sable Shetland Sheepdog ("Sheltie") who lived to be 15, and took excellent care of her master, a retired CPA in Denver named Radleigh Valentine.

When I was growing up, my aunt had Shelties, which is probably the reason I am particularly drawn to this breed. One day I decided to look at a litter of Sheltie puppies, in hopes of finding the right one to be my companion. Only one puppy jumped up and showed an interest in me. Her name was Lindsey, and she had been taken into other homes, only to be returned for one or two of the various reasons why people suddenly find dogs inconvenient. Perhaps the children developed allergies, or the family wanted a bigger dog to roughhouse with, or the elderly couple decided to move to an apartment. Shuffled back and forth, the little pup was dubbed "Boomerang Lindsey." This time was different. Lindsey chose me, and remained with me for the rest of her life.

Even as an adult, Lindsey was quite small. Actually, she was the tiniest Sheltie I'd ever seen! Lindsey's smallness only added to her elegance. She was always graceful and regal in her demeanor and would lie down and cross her little white paws, one over the other, just as any refined lady would do. One could picture her in a fancy hat and white gloves, ready to go out to tea. I christened her with a new nickname: "Her Highness." Friends would bow and offer homage to "Her Highness" whenever they came into my home. And since I was totally overprotective of her, my friends called me "Sir Radleigh, the Paranoid." Lindsey loved company and always knew when friends were coming over, even when I didn't. For no apparent reason, she would start barking and sit by the door. I would smile whenever I saw her do that...and sure enough, the doorbell would ring.

For 14 years I took on the self-assigned role of shepherding, protecting, and guiding my elegant little dog. As time went on, however, I came to realize with some embarrassment that it was actually she who was guiding, protecting, and shepherding me. My bond with Lindsey grew tremendously as the years passed, even to the point of regarding her as my spirit guide. As Lindsey grew older, her liver and kidneys began to fail. Late one evening, I took her to the emergency clinic, realizing that the end was near. As her condition deteriorated, her heart gave out from exhaustion, and she passed away early the next morning. I was with her at the clinic until shortly before she died, and I was so grateful that she had died on her own and I did not have to make the decision to euthanize her. It was Lindsey's gift to me, her final act of love, but that did not ease my grief. Even though I had anticipated the loss of my little girl and special companion, it was emotionally traumatic and hard to accept.

Within a week after Lindsey's passing, I started seeing her in my peripheral vision. It seemed strange to see her that way. I would have to remind myself that she was gone. These episodes usually occurred when I was moving about the house, busy doing everyday chores, and not thinking of her.

By the second week, my reaction changed when I saw her. I would stop, cover my eyes (I don't know why), and talk to her. Several times, I caught a glimpse of her around my feet, which caused me to trip. These episodes lingered into the third week after her passing, and then gradually disappeared.

Later on, Lindsey frequently contacted me with synchronistic episodes. One day I went to buy some items for the kitchen. The saleswoman introduced herself as Lindsey. On my way home, I saw a couple walking a small, sable Sheltie that looked very much like my Lindsey. Then I discovered a flyer tucked into my door – from Lindsey Painting Company. When I first saw the flyer, only the word "LINDSEY" was prominent, written in large, bold letters. I could imagine my beloved Sheltie saying to me, "Do you get it _yet_?"

On my computer I have a Ceiva frame, which rotates and displays 20 pictures in a specific order. One picture is of Lindsey. One day as I was going through my e-mail, I noticed an unsolicited message with the name "Lindsey" in it. At that exact moment, the Ceiva frame moved to Lindsey's picture!

Many other occurrences have let me know that Lindsey is still around me. Often I feel her presence, precious and profound, especially when I am remembering our years together and wishing I could see her again. Her nearness is palpable. I feel extremely comforted, humbled, and touched that she has contacted me so many times since her passing. She keeps conveying to me the fact that I am not alone. I believe she is committed to staying with me for my lifetime, waiting to meet me on the Other Side.

I have always believed that pets possess a soul and experience an afterlife. Although I didn't think much about it before Lindsey passed away, my belief in these matters has deepened considerably. Without a doubt, Lindsey remains with me in spirit. Her ashes are housed in a beautiful oak box, kept by my bed.

A side note from graphic artist Zee Marie of Zee Designs: While I was typing this story of Lindsey for Dr. Redding, an amazing series of synchronistic events happened to me in my office. My partner handed me a piece of mail, which had the name "Lindsay" on it. Within moments, I received e-mail from "Lindsey" and immediately after that, I got a phone call from "Lindsay." By this time, goose bumps were running up and down my arms! The spelling of the name may have varied slightly, but I could only wonder if Radleigh's beloved Sheltie was trying to contact me.

Dee Dee

...a Dalmatian who lived for 13 years with Julie Kemp, an obedience and agility dog trainer in California.

I first saw Dee Dee on the day I was hoping to buy a beautiful dog to be shown in conformation. The lady selling the Dalmatian puppies pointed out the best choice, which happened to be the only puppy who was not paying any attention to me! While the other members of the litter were trying desperately to win me over, my future show dog was busy sniffing around nonchalantly and playing with toys. Once I picked her up, though, she seemed so sweet and affectionate I quickly forgot her previous indifference. I just had to have her!

As fate would have it, Dee Dee did not grow up to be of show quality. Undaunted by this discovery, I decided to train her in obedience, but obedience didn't seem to be her thing, either. With her independent attitude, she was difficult to motivate and teach. She showed little interest in doing the exercises until I got the idea of using a tennis ball in her practice sessions. Using the ball definitely helped her jumping, retrieving, and heeling, but not those stationary exercises that demanded she remain lying down or sitting for some time. Dee Dee still loved to sniff! If a scent caught her attention, she would forget what she should be doing and move out of position. After overcoming many difficulties, I finally showed her, and she performed surprisingly well in

her novice trials. But when we started competing for a more advanced title and probably after she figured out that we were not going to play ball, her focus and performance deteriorated. In a moment of desperation, I told her, "Dee Dee, you'd better do well at this show or you will be staying home for the rest of your life!" That seemed to shake her up a bit. She finished her CDX (Companion Dog Excellent) title that day.

Although Dee Dee got along with my husband and children, everybody knew that she was really my dog. Despite her independence, she had become very attached to me and always wanted to be with me. I usually took her if I went somewhere, but when I left for my part-time evening job, Dee Dee knew she had to stay home. As soon as I put on my perfume, she would retire to her crate in the kitchen and stay there until I returned. On Saturdays when I worked all day, Dee Dee followed the same routine. My kids would try to coax her to come out of her crate to play, but she would not budge. When I got home, everything changed. Dee Dee was happy again, and always dashed out to greet me enthusiastically. Without a doubt, we had a special bond.

When Dee Dee was ten, she became deaf in both ears, which is quite common for Dalmatians. Later her health deteriorated and she developed kidney failure. When she finally stopped eating and lost the ability to walk, I knew that it was time to have her euthanized. It was such a sad day. My daughter, Samantha, and I took her to the vet. We stayed with her during the procedure and for some time afterward.

About a month later, Samantha had an amazing experience. This is her description of what happened:

While my mom was taking her customary bath around eleven at night, I walked toward the closed bathroom door to tell her something. On the floor next to the bathroom door, I saw Dee Dee! She was lying in the place where she always waited for my mom. I saw her clearly, so much so that I had to walk over her to get close to the door. Even after I stepped over her, she was still in the way and making it awkward for me to get close to the door. I looked down and told her to move. Nothing seemed out of the ordinary until I realized that Dee Dee shouldn't be there! She was dead! Just as I thought this, her image began to fade into the carpet. For a few seconds, I could still see her outline, but then that also disappeared. I moved my foot over the place where she had been resting. Nothing was there. Afterward I cried, even though I felt exhilarated at the same time.

About a month after Samantha's experience, I had contact with Dee Dee. It happened on a Sunday, about eight in the morning, while the rest of my family was still asleep. We now had two dogs, Buddy and Music. I was alone in the living room with Music, who was just a puppy. I was sitting in the quiet house when I suddenly and distinctly heard doggy footsteps in the kitchen. Thinking Buddy might need to go outside, I went to the kitchen to let him out. Buddy wasn't there. Then I remembered he was sleeping in my son's bedroom. My son always has his door closed at this time of day. His room has wall-to-wall carpeting and is located at least 20 feet from the kitchen. Since the sound obviously could not have come from either Buddy or Music, I believe I heard Dee Dee. Samantha agrees. She thinks Dee Dee stayed around to watch over me while I was grieving. Both of us believe that our pets exist in some form after death, and that we will see them again in the afterlife.

Ginger

...a sweet little Dachshund who lived to be 16, but who no doubt poured most of her living into her final year of life, when she was befriended by Riesa Larson, a medical receptionist whose hobby is rescuing and taking care of animals.

All my life I have loved animals and have taken care of them, but a little Dachshund, colored like cinnamon and named Ginger, made the most lasting impression on me. She was an old dog, 15 years when I first became acquainted with her. Even more amazing, she did not belong to me. Her owners were two doctors, a husband and wife. At the time I met the dog, I had just begun to work as a medical receptionist for the husband. The building where I was working served as both his office and his home.

Shortly after I started my new job, I became aware of a dog whimpering behind the husband's office door. I soon discovered that it was the doctor's little dog Ginger, who was left alone most of the day. One day I went into the house to see her. Although I have never been particularly attracted to Dachshunds, I loved Ginger from the moment I saw her. She was so friendly, affectionate, and grateful for my attention that she touched my heart. Before long, I started visiting her on a regular basis. Holding and petting her made me feel wonderful because I knew I was giving her the attention she craved. I also frequently trimmed her nails, which had grown very long. After some time, her owner allowed me to bring her into the office while I was working. Wearing a "big smile," she would sit on my lap and lick my face. My co-worker thought it was disgusting that I would let a dog kiss me. She had no clue about the close relationship Ginger and I were sharing.

In a few months, I had the doctor's permission to take his little Dachshund for a walk after work. As evening approached, Ginger became very excited as she anticipated our walk together. I can see her now with her joyous expression, moving her little feet rapidly, clicking and clacking her nails against the floor. Knowing that she was so happy filled me with such joy that I felt a spiritual connection to her. Ginger was now my "soul mate."

Eventually I was allowed to take her home with me at night, and then I would bring her back to the office when I returned to work in the morning. We spent a lot of our evenings together cuddling on the sofa. If my cats tried to sit next to me, the little dog would chase them away, as if to say, "This is MY turn with her!" I'll never forget the way Ginger looked up at me. Her gaze was enchanting, and I tried to memorize it to hold in my heart forever. When the weather grew colder, I bought her a little purple sweater. She looked absolutely adorable in it! This idyllic time of togetherness, taking her for walks and taking her home with me at night, lasted for seven months.

Then suddenly, without warning, the doctor decided I was "spoiling her." He no longer allowed me to take her for evening walks, or to take her home to spend the night with me. Worse than that, I was not permitted to keep her with me in the office. Ginger was returned to being isolated behind the office door. I was devastated. All day long, I could hear her whimpering in the adjoining room. The situation was almost unbearable. Whenever I got a chance, I would sneak into the house to give her some love and attention. My boss and my co-worker could not understand or share my feelings. To them, Ginger was just a "pain in the neck." Our separation continued in this way for five months, until I broke my arm on April 23. Now temporarily at home and unable to visit Ginger, I worried that she would feel deserted, unhappy, and lonely, and that as a result, she might become ill and die. I prayed over and over again that she would manage to survive until I returned.

On May 8, I could not get her off my mind. I was totally preoccupied with worrying about her. That evening, my husband and I attended a concert, but I didn't enjoy it. All during the concert, I was quietly weeping. I couldn't understand why I suddenly missed her so much!

The next day, as I was tossing a ball for my big Lab, I heard a series of distinct, high-pitched barks, which obviously came from a small dog. "Isn't that weird," I asked myself, as I looked around, trying to determine their source. It occurred to me that it sounded like Ginger's bark, but I quickly dismissed that idea, deciding that I had imagined the sounds because I was missing her.

Two days later, my boss called to see how I was doing. I told him how much I missed Ginger, and asked him to please bring her to my house so that I could see her. He agreed. Soon I heard a knock at the door and ran eagerly to see my little friend. As I opened the door, I saw the doctor's daughter, but there was no sign of the dog. The daughter informed me reluctantly that Ginger had passed away four days earlier, on May 7. She had died peacefully in their backyard, wearing the purple sweater I had bought for her.

I was stunned and heartbroken, but I realized that somehow I must have known that she was gone. That was the reason I kept thinking about her the day after she died, and why I had wept all through the concert. Then I remembered that I had heard her barking, only to dismiss it as my imagination. Now I believe that she was trying to communicate with me.

My grief and guilt tormented me. Did my little girl die because I went away? Did she think I had deserted her, and didn't love her anymore? Did she die of a broken heart? I deeply regretted not being with her during those last two weeks. My only consolation was that when she died, she was wearing the purple sweater I had given her. At least a part of me had been with her at the end. I put her picture next to my bed. Every night I cried and prayed that she would visit me in a dream. Days passed and nothing happened. Then, exactly one month after her death, my prayers were answered. Ginger came to visit me in an exquisitely vivid dream. I don't usually remember my dreams, but this one was different. Every detail is still perfectly clear, as if it were a real experience.

In my dream, Ginger came and sat next to me, and I could feel her little body pressing against mine. She appeared healthy and very excited to be with me again. For some reason, I left momentarily to speak to someone, but remembering her, I came back. When I picked her up, I could feel the weight of her in my arms, as though she were really there. I felt the same deep connection to her, and knew that we would always love one another. When I awoke, I felt elated. I was certain that she had visited me, and I couldn't wait to tell my friends the good news.

My sadness and guilt returned again, but to a lesser degree. Somehow, Ginger had understood that I wanted to be with her at the end. We had shared 14 wonderful months together, and had packed a lifetime of love into those short days. I thank God that He gave me a chance to bring some comfort and joy into the last year of her life.

> "The way a person treats an animal is an index to his soul."
>
> … Rabbinical Proverb

Pumpkin

...a Golden Retriever who lived in Texas for 12 years with a church administrative assistant, Linda C. Himes, whose hobbies include reading, writing, painting, and "probably more to come."

After living alone in a cottage with three cats, I began to think that a large dog would be a good addition to my family. One evening while I was driving to work in my rural community, I happened upon a beautiful, but very thin Golden Retriever. He was resting comfortably in the middle of the road, looking over the headlights as if to say, "Well, here I am...your big dog!" It took a few days before his message began to sink in. I saw him frequently for several weeks, but was never able to pick him up because I was always on my way to work.

One morning, my friend Betty showed up at my house, proclaiming, "Wake up! I've got the perfect dog for you!" I quickly jumped into some clothes and went out to her truck. There, wriggling on his back and

wagging his tail to beat the band, was my Golden Retriever friend. We took him out of the truck, gave him food and water, and watched his delirious joy in our presence. Then we noticed he wasn't alone! Millions of huge, voracious fleas were hopping all over him, and who knows how long they had been traveling together! After several baths and treatments, my big dog was ready to come home. I called him Pumpkin.

He paid no attention to my three cats as he walked into the house. The cats, on the other hand, seemed a bit concerned — understandably so, since they had previously endured a Pit Bull puppy in a three-story walkup flat in San Francisco. Each cat scrutinized Pumpkin carefully and then looked at the others as if to agree, "This guy doesn't look too bad." Pumpkin's age was difficult to determine, but I guessed that he was about six. I soon discovered that he was infected with heartworm, which required immediate treatment. It was clear from his overall condition that he had been on his own for a long time.

My mom dearly loved our newest addition to the family, which was a surprise, considering his questionable background. Mother was a proper, conservative perfectionist who was always impeccably dressed. Her favorite piece of furniture was an antique brocade-covered Queen Anne couch that her mother had given to her. My mother would sit on her sofa and invite Pumpkin to join her. He would galumph up next to her and put his head in her lap, and they would cuddle like that for hours.

Toward the end of his life, Pumpkin developed megaesophagus, a condition that results in vomiting, aspiration of food, and often in pneumonia. Two months after the diagnosis, I knew that he could not be healed, and that his illness could not be managed effectively. Realizing that he would have to leave me soon, I asked Pumpkin to send me another perfect dog, just like him. When the time came, he laid his sweet face in the crook of my arm and peacefully let go of his life as the merciful shot was given. I was devastated afterward, but I recovered gradually and returned to the rhythm of living.

Two months after Pumpkin's passing, I felt that I was ready to get another dog. Having a hunch, I looked in the classified section of the paper, something I had never done before. There I found an ad for a six-year-old male Golden at an unbelievably low price. I called several times but got no answer. After these futile attempts, I decided that this probably wasn't the dog for me, but I continued to think about the dog throughout the night. The next morning when I walked into the bathroom, I glanced up at the little snapshot of Pumpkin that had been sitting on the shelf for nearly a year. Plop! It fell over at the exact moment I looked at it. There was no open window, no wind, and no reason at all for it to move! "Okay, Pumpkin! I'm going!" I said. I called the number again, and this time, I got right through. I jumped into the car, drove 60 miles, and found my new dog, a huge, gorgeous Golden Retriever! He was so sweet I called him "Sugar Bear." He turned out to be Pumpkin's perfect gift, and we have been together now for three years.

But that wasn't the only time I heard from Pumpkin. After he died, my vet sent me some wonderfully fragrant potpourri, which I placed in a dish above the head of my bed. For some time the scent was sweetly present, but after a couple of months I would have to shake it and sprinkle it with water to evoke the odor. Much later, on four separate occasions, the unmistakable fragrance of the potpourri spontaneously filled the room and lingered longer than usual. Even if I left the room and then returned after some time, the scent would still be detectable. I smelled the potpourri distinctly on the first anniversary of Pumpkin's death! On the other three occasions, I was relaxing in my bedroom late in the day. Each time I sensed Pumpkin's presence and experienced an evanescent sighting of him out of the corner of my eye. I recognized his color and movement and caught a glimpse of his form traveling around the side of my bed. It could not have been Sugar Bear, because he was always asleep next to me. Miss Girl, my only cat, was nestled in my lap. Each time, I felt a rush of joy and knew that Pumpkin was "checking in," so to speak. I always made a point of telling him "Hi!" and of talking to him a bit about things we could remember together.

I believe every being has a soul, and that we are connected forever to the ones we love. Pumpkin's happy little visits seem to corroborate my beliefs. When my mother died of congestive heart failure, I had several recurring dreams in which I saw her together with Pumpkin. Mother always appeared healthy and happy, as did Pumpkin. They adored each other, and it is fitting that they should now be together to share the afterlife.

Jaxx and *K.C.*

...two Doberman Pinschers who loved each other and played together until Jaxx died suddenly when he was not quite seven years old. They owned Elina Heine, a physical therapist in southern California, whose hobbies are cycling, hiking, swimming, and dog agility.

A few years ago, I had an astonishing experience, which at first, I found difficult to accept. When I did accept it, I came to believe that it confirmed the existence of our pets after they die. It also taught me a lesson about respecting an animal's feelings.

My friend Carla and I owned a two-year-old female Doberman and called her K.C. for her dark brown coat, which reminded us of Kona coffee. My story begins when we were looking for a canine companion for her. That's when a male Doberman, whom we named Jaxx, came into our lives. He was a ten-month-old rescue dog with hardly any hair on the outside and an infestation of three types of worms on the inside. Although he had a large frame, he weighed only 40 pounds, as he had obviously been feeding the worms as well as himself! The two dogs hit it off immediately. They had no more than said hello before they were chasing each other, doing body slams, and roughhousing everywhere from the backyard to the inside of the house.

Despite their closeness, their temperaments were very different. Jaxx was gentle, needy, and affectionate. His favorite thing was sitting on our laps, even though he weighed 70 pounds once his health was restored! K.C., on the other hand, was the ultimate, first-class bitch, extremely controlling and aloof. If she became aware that Jaxx wanted to snuggle with her, she would refuse his affection. That didn't stop Jaxx, who would lay his head tenderly on her

foot. There were those rare occasions when both of them occupied the same wicker basket, with Jaxx wearing an expression of beatific joy!

As much as they enjoyed snuggling, both dogs loved action even more. We trained them in agility, with my friend Carla running Jaxx while I ran K.C. For several years, Carla and I did agility demonstrations for the Pooch Parade, a yearly event to benefit a local dog rescue organization. The dogs ran side by side on two parallel courses, testing both the speed of the dogs and the skill of their handlers. At least this was the intention. Many times, however, Jaxx's joie de vivre would cause him to bolt from his course and leap into mine to play with K.C. That's all it took for both dogs to get completely out of control and act like total goofballs, running through the same tunnel or taking the same jump together. The crowd roared with delight, cheering them on with enthusiasm. Jaxx and K.C. came to be known as the "Dynamic Dobie Duo."

For six years, Jaxx and K.C. remained close companions, active and healthy. Carla frequently took Jaxx jogging with her, something he always looked forward to. One evening while Carla was running with him, Jaxx suddenly dropped dead, apparently from cardiac arrest. There had never been any inkling of a heart problem, but perhaps the worms and poor nutrition during those early months damaged him in ways we could not have known.

Poor Carla! In addition to the terrible shock of Jaxx's death, she was faced with the problem of how to get this big dog home. Fortunately, a passerby agreed to help and put Jaxx into the back of his truck. While all this was happening, I was at home, happily preparing dinner and completely oblivious of what Carla was going through.

Since our Dobies seemed healthy and were relatively young, Carla and I had never discussed what to do if one of them died. Consequently, we were totally unprepared for this event. What do you do when a 70-pound dog dies at 7:30 in the evening? I made a spur-of-the-moment decision to take Jaxx's body to the animal shelter for immediate disposal. I also made a point of not allowing K.C. or our little Border Collie Turbo see Jaxx's body because I wanted to "protect" them.

It was customary for K.C. to wake me up at three o'clock in the morning to let her go outside. I could have set my clock by her habit. She would make a low, groaning noise until I got out of bed, and then we always walked directly from the bedroom to the back door. The night after Jaxx's death, *everything* changed dramatically. K.C. woke me as usual, but she was uttering an unusually loud, pitiful whining sound, one I had never heard before. Thinking she needed to go outside, I got up and followed her as she continued to behave strangely. Instead of walking straight to the back door, she began to wander throughout the house, going in and out of every room, all the while making this peculiar, stricken noise. "What in the world is wrong?" I wondered.

The next night, the same thing happened, and then it happened again the following night, and *all* the nights after that for just over a month! Although it finally occurred to me that she was in mourning and trying to find Jaxx, I didn't know what to do about it. I tried to console her, but it didn't seem to have any effect. Eventually her whining diminished, but her roaming throughout the house continued.

Then, exactly three months to the day after Jaxx's passing, an incredible thing happened. K.C. woke me up with a sad, moaning whine, and I braced myself for another despondent, fruitless walk through the rooms of our house. This time, however, instead of roaming around, she walked briskly down the hallway while I followed behind her. As soon as she got to the entrance of the living room, she stopped abruptly and turned her head. She stood motionless, staring into the living room, which was dimly lit by an outside porch light. I turned to see what had caught her eye. It was Jaxx, looking at us! He was lying on his bed, the one I had left beside my chair. I saw him so plainly...and apparently, so did K.C.! After a few moments, I sensed that K.C. was looking up at me, so I glanced down at her. Our eyes met and we had a moment of profound silent communication. I knew she was telling me, "See, there's Jaxx. I found him and he is okay."

Afterward, I felt a tremendous sense of calm as K.C. and I walked back to the bedroom. I knew that K.C.

had experienced some closure. I realized that our relationships with our canine friends endure beyond our time together in this physical world, as do our relationships with the people we have loved and lost. In the preceding weeks, I had learned the importance of respecting a dog's feelings when a close canine pal dies. In a broader sense, I now understood the importance of ceremonies that people use to honor the dead. It is important to both people and animals to have the opportunity to say goodbye.

By the morning, however, my serenity had turned to disbelief. How could I have seen Jaxx alive? It made no sense to my rational brain. I decided that I must have dreamt the whole thing. "What a dream I had!" I told Carla. Yet down deep, I knew it wasn't a dream.

Consumed by my conflict, I was quiet and preoccupied at work the next day. A dear Hawaiian friend and co-worker picked up on my mood and asked me what was wrong. There was no way I was going to tell her that my dead dog had appeared in my living room at three o'clock in the morning! I wondered how to answer her, but then without any prompting, my spiritual friend said, "Jaxx visited you, didn't he?" Her insight stunned me, but it also encouraged me to share my story. After recounting the events, my friend told me that according to Hawaiian culture, when a loved one dies and there are unresolved issues, the spirit returns in an attempt to remedy the situation. Her words were so consoling they enabled me to accept and understand this extraordinary event as a true afterlife visitation!

After K.C. saw Jaxx that night, her peculiar whines and nightly tours of the house stopped abruptly. Her "memorial service" had ended. We all slept well after that, secure in the knowledge that Jaxx existed peacefully in the afterlife.

A few weeks later, I came across the collar Jaxx used to wear. That evening, as I was packing for an agility trial, I held it up, and Carla and I made a toast to Jaxx. With K.C. and our Border Collie Turbo standing nearby, I said, "Cheers to all our canine friends, past, present, and future!" We drank some great wine, and fed each of the dogs a cookie. We dedicated the next day's trial to Jaxx. And what a day it was! Both dogs qualified in their runs and won first place, each time! Four first-place ribbons in one day out of four runs. Unbelievable! I've made it a point to say that same toast before other trials, but never again has it carried the same luck as it did that special day. But that did not stop us from still drinking a bit of wine and letting the dogs munch on cookies to remember all our canine friends and the joy they have given us.

When it was time to put K.C. down, I knew better than to make the same mistake twice! Our wonderful holistic vet came to our home, and K.C. passed away peacefully in our arms, in the garden. Our two remaining dogs, Turbo and Jeff, took the opportunity to say goodbye in their own canine way. Afterward, we had no mournful cries, no late-night wanderings through the house. And even though we have had no more visitations from Jaxx, and none from K.C., we know that they are still with us.

Sam

...a mixture of Poodle and Pug who had the best of each, Sam lived in Nebraska with Bernice Halsey, the mother of Laura. Laura Halsey wrote, "My mother died some years ago. I grew up with her beloved Sam and remember him well. I'd like to share her story, just as I think my mother would tell it.'

When I first saw Sam, he was standing on his hind legs in a little cage at the pet shop. Sam's front feet pushed through the wire with his toes spread so far apart that he appeared to be hanging on the side of his cage. He looked straight at me with his adorable big eyes that seemed to say, "Look how cute I am. You have to take me!" Whenever my family and I turned away to consider another puppy, Sam would start whining, as though pleading, "Oh, please don't leave me!" Sam, of course, was the pup we chose to take home.

"Sam" H
pug / poo

Sam, who had short black hair, grew up to be a very energetic, athletic little guy. He loved to run and was able to perform incredibly athletic moves that took my breath away. In addition, he had a lovely, gentle disposition and was friendly to everyone. His tail and rear end would wag back and forth whenever he greeted us, and he would pull his lips back into a big grin. We all referred to him as "Sweet Pea Sam" because of his loving and sensitive nature. Only once did Sam become ferociously protective, barking and lunging at a stranger who stopped and asked Laura for directions while she was raking leaves. There was something about the man that frightened Laura, who was at home alone. Sensing my daughter's fear, Sam saw to it that the intruder left quickly!

Sweet Pea Sam followed me wherever I went, and if I was reading, he would cuddle up as close as possible.

I was forever talking to my little guy, often asking, "Sam, where is your baby?" As soon as he heard those words, he would scamper away to pick up a soft toy and bring it to me. Then Sam would collapse with the toy under his chin, looking up at me with his big, beautiful eyes, and my heart would melt. Although he loved to rest in my lap, at night he ran to his own bed and waited for a little treat before "lights out"!

For seven years, Sam was the joy of my life, until one day when he literally fell over, as if he were having a seizure. Afterward, he appeared to be confused, and staggered when he walked. It was shocking to see such a young dog in that condition, especially as he had been so healthy and energetic up to that moment. We rushed him to the vet, who discovered extensive damage to Sam's heart, possibly caused by parasites. He was given medications and for a short time, he seemed to improve. We tried to keep him calm and quiet, but having restrictions on his activity only made him unhappy.

A few weeks after the first incident, Sam fell over again and was unable to use his hind legs. We rushed him back to the vet, who said Sam had probably suffered a stroke, and warned us that his health would continue to deteriorate. The paralysis in his legs was permanent. I thought it would be selfish to keep Sam alive. For the sake of my little dog, I decided to have him euthanized. As the solution was administered, I cradled him lovingly in my arms. Later, I sobbed and brought his body home for burial in our backyard. Over and over, I wondered if I had done the right thing.

Three days after Sam was euthanized, I was in the kitchen washing dishes when I heard the sound of dog tags clinking against the water bowl. *Clink, clink, clink.* "Oh, Sam must be out of water," I thought absently. Then I realized that wasn't possible, and I dismissed the sounds as being my imagination. Moments later, I heard the "clinking" noise again. This time it seemed to be coming from the porch. I left the kitchen to investigate, but as soon as I stepped outside, the clinking sound stopped. Now, certain that I had heard dog tags, I wondered if I might see Sam, and although I didn't see him, I believe he was there.

That night, I was awakened by the same "clinking" noise. Half asleep, I got out of bed, thinking Sam needed water. *Clink, clink, clink*, I kept hearing as I walked in a haze to the kitchen. By the time I got there, it dawned on me once again that Sam was no longer alive. Nevertheless, I turned on the light to search for him, and I called out for him several times. By this time, there was no way I could chalk up those sounds to pure imagination. I'm sure I heard them!

The next evening, my daughter, Laura, came running excitedly to tell me she had seen Sam! She had just come home, and was taking off her riding boots in the basement as usual. When Sam was alive, he would stand in the middle of the basement stairs, watching Laura remove her boots. Then Laura would run up the stairs and give him a big hug. This time, however, Laura thought she was alone; but when she looked up she caught Sam's reflection in one of the mirrors in the basement, hung there for her ballet practice. "Hi, Sammy!" she said without thinking. Then it hit her. Sammy was gone. Startled, Laura looked behind her right shoulder to see him, but he wasn't there. Then she glanced back to the mirror, but his reflection was gone. My daughter told me that Sam appeared healthy and happy. He was wagging his tail, with his whole body shaking, just as it used to when he greeted her. She remembered, too, that his lips were pulled back in that characteristic smile. Laura wasn't alone after all – Sam was still there, watching her as always.

I felt comforted and relieved when I heard Sam's dog tags, and when Laura told me that she had seen him. I wasn't surprised because Sam adored my daughter. I felt great joy to hear that our precious little dog was happy and healthy in the afterlife. I believe animals are pure, and have a kind of innocence that keeps them close to God. Perhaps they are actually the Lord's favored ones, here to teach us about joy, honesty, reliability, gratitude, unconditional love, and living in the moment.

My mother's love for Sam touched our hearts. I feel sure that she and Sam are together again, joyful and close to God.

...Laura Halsey

Korkie

...a Shetland Sheepdog who spent his 16 years with Diane Tyioran, a dog trainer and competitor in obedience.

When I was 13, I endured a traumatic event that tainted my outlook on people and life in general. I became very cynical and did not believe in God or Heaven or life after death. All that changed years later, when my Sheltie came to visit me after he died. This dog is responsible for changing my beliefs and bringing me renewed happiness, optimism, and peace. Now I know that pets do exist after death, and I believe that people do, too.

It was my brother-in-law who saw an ad in the paper for Sheltie puppies. I had been grieving over the loss of my dog, Koko, who had died after 17 years. Everyone was encouraging me to get another pet. After seeing the ad, my sister, my mother, and I went to inspect the litter. One pup stood out as the leader. The little guy was active, fearless, and full of himself, while the other puppies dutifully followed him wherever he went. I wanted a male, so I chose the bold one and called him Korkie.

Because we lived close to several busy streets, I was concerned for the safety of my rambunctious puppy, so I took him to an obedience class as soon as possible. I really enjoyed the training sessions, and before long, they became an important part of my life. Although Korkie was a good sport in class and understood quickly what was expected of him, he was strong-willed and accustomed to being the boss. Consequently, he did some of the exercises in rather unconventional ways. I affectionately dubbed his unique behaviors "Korkie's Quirks." If I tried to change his method, he would simply refuse to do the exercises. It was his way or no way at all!

The scent exercise begins with the handler's putting his scent on one of 12 articles by rubbing it between his hands. The dog must find the scented object and bring it back to his handler, who stands about 20 feet away. Most dogs locate the proper item by methodically sniffing each one...but not Korkie. He would dash out and run frantically around the pile. Again and again he would circle it, until suddenly he would dive in and grab the correct article. The judge and all the people watching were amazed, and wondered how he could consistently choose the right item without actually smelling it.

His "stand for examination" exercise was also done in an unconventional manner, to say the least! In this exercise, the handler leaves the dog in a standing position, while the judge runs his hands over the dog from its head to the rear. If the dog moves, he loses points. Korkie rarely moved, but he would lean as far away from the judge as possible, turn his head, and look in the opposite direction, as if to say, "I am so disgusted that you are *touching* me. How much longer do I have to endure this?" It is a wonder that he never fell over! His behavior is easy to understand when you realize that Korkie was never an overly friendly or affectionate dog, even with me. He would do *anything* for me, but being demonstrative was not in his nature. After all, he was a macho little dog with an image to maintain, and the Sheltie standard insists that while the dog must be loyal and responsive to his owner, he may be reserved and aloof to strangers, but never fearful. Keeping that in mind, Korkie was an excellent example of the breed!

Despite his peculiarities, Korkie excelled in obedience, and earned his Utility Dog title along with many blue ribbons by the time he was ten. I was so proud of him, and felt that he truly lived up to his registered name, Korkie The Korker U.D. When he was over 15, he was honored as the oldest Sheltie ever to place in an obedience trial at the ASSA National Specialty Show. His accomplishments were published in several magazines, including the *American Kennel Club Gazette*.

Korkie helped me raise and train Zack, an abused Sheltie that I adopted. Zack was about two when I rescued him, and he turned out to be more of a problem than I had expected. He was an hysterical little Sheltie, constantly running, barking, and freaking out over everything, even to the point of foaming at his mouth. Thank goodness for Korkie, who took it upon himself to be the protector and trainer of this problem child. If I called Zack and he ignored me, Korkie would come to the rescue by cornering him and herding him in my direction. If another dog threatened Zack, Korkie would place himself between Zack and the danger. One day, I was frustrated with little Zack and went to scold him. Korkie knew I was angry, and stood between Zack and me. He even growled to warn me not to hurt him. I realized that Korkie was right, and backed off.

Eventually Korkie and I managed to train Zack in obedience so that he earned his Utility Dog title, a rather amazing accomplishment. Whenever I showed the dogs together, everyone referred to them affectionately as "the Brace Boys." If Zack lagged behind, Korkie would nip him as a reminder to keep up. If Zack moved too far away from me, Korkie would push him back into position. It was always Korkie who was the boss and kept both Zack and me in line!

Korkie remained robust and healthy until he neared the end of his life. Shortly after his 16th birthday, he was diagnosed with an autoimmune disease. Over the next three months, his illness became worse. Considering his age and the poor quality of his life, I decided to have him euthanized. During the procedure, I remained with him to be of some comfort. Once he was gone, I cried for days. I was so overwhelmed with grief I thought I might be losing my mind. Zack was 13 then, and had many health problems. Because I knew that he needed me, I managed to go on, one day at a time.

About a year after Korkie died, he surprised me by coming back to visit while I was taking an afternoon nap. I had not even been thinking of him that day. I suppose, technically, my encounter was a dream, but I had never experienced a dream like this one. Perhaps I had an "out of body experience" because it felt as real as anything that had ever happened to me. In any case, I have no doubt that Korkie was actually with me.

As it happened, I was standing in my front yard, which faces a busy street. I suddenly saw Korkie watching me from the other side. As our eyes met, I knew he would try to come to me. "No, Korkie! Stop! Stay there!

I'll come and get you," I shouted, with tears streaming down my face. But Korkie kept running, never taking his eyes off me. A van approached from one direction and a car from the other. Both drivers slammed on their brakes to avoid hitting my dog. Korkie must have been aware of the vehicles, but he was on a mission, and determined to get to me no matter what the danger. It was typical of him not to let anything stand in his way. Once he reached me, my tears continued, but they were tears of joy. Korkie's eyes were dark brown and beautifully expressive, just as I remembered. He was jumping up and down so much that I could hardly touch him. As he jumped, he barked in his unique, deep voice. I kept telling him how good he looked, recalling that before he passed away, he had been very thin. Now he was strong and muscular, his sturdy self again! Eventually he settled down enough for me to pet him. I remember touching and feeling him as if he were alive. We were together again for a few brief moments. Then he was gone.

I had to take a moment to catch my breath. My face was covered with tears as I got up from my nap, emotionally exhausted and shocked by what had occurred. I spent the rest of the day in a daze, pondering and reliving it all. Eventually I understood that Korkie had come from the Other Side to deliver important messages to me. He returned to let me know that he had been healed and rejuvenated. He wanted to reassure me that our bond of love was eternal, and that he would be waiting for me. It moved me to realize how much he loved me. Korkie had always been a source of strength for me, and he still continued that role in the afterlife.

Although seven years have passed, I can still picture our reunion as if it had just happened. The memory never leaves me. I think about it almost every day. I needed only one experience to convince me that Korkie still exists, and that there is life after death for pets as well as people.

Years ago, when Korkie was just three, my sister purchased a large, very realistic figurine of a Sheltie, and called it "Korkie's Statue." I put it in my front yard on a bed of gravel. For 20 years, nothing grew around it. Then suddenly, in the summer just after I talked to Dr. Redding about my story, I was shocked to see a flowering plant sprouting next to the statue! The plant lived a long time, even with the advent of cold weather. I believe it was a sign from my beloved Korkie, who is pleased that I have chosen to share his story.

Basil

...a beloved Welsh Terrier who lived 14 years in California with Laurie Fisher, an interpreter of sign language.

My husband and I were childless, so I thought it would be nice to get a dog. Before I was married, I had owned an Airedale, whom I dearly loved, but this time I wanted a smaller dog with the same characteristics. When I saw a picture of a Welsh Terrier, I knew exactly what breed my new dog would be. I approached my husband, who seemed quite resistant to adding a dog to our family. "A *dog*," he grumbled. "You don't *really* want a dog, do you?"

"Well," I replied, "it's a dog or it's a baby. Take your choice." My husband opted for the dog!

Soon we went to see our first litter of Welsh Terrier puppies. Since we were going only to look, and had no intention of buying, we brought no checkbook, leash, collar, or kennel. There were two males left, and we spent several hours playing with them, quite a long time for people who were not intending to purchase a pup. The owner encouraged us to take the friendlier puppy, but I had my mind set on the independent one. In any case, the owner was most eager to sell us either little fellow, so much so that he took only $75 in cash and agreed that we could send him the balance later. He also supplied us with a collar, leash, and even a kennel for our new companion!

We named our new dog Basil. He was an energetic, three-month-old rascal, who loved to chase a tennis ball, but never thought about bringing it back. He enjoyed tug-o-war also, and this was a game we could play together. Basil's favorite tug toy was a teddy bear that was three times his size. My husband and I would get down on the floor and entice him to play. Before long, Basil would be growling, attacking, and trying to pull the bear out of our hands. He played with reckless enthusiasm, until, suddenly exhausted, he would stumble into his kennel and plop down to take a nap. At this point nothing could coax him out of his bed. It wasn't long before my husband absolutely adored our new puppy.

Basil was a typical Welsh Terrier, full of himself and friendly to everyone — except toddlers, whom he ignored. Perhaps he felt threatened by their "cuteness" and the attention they always received, which he felt was rightly his own. His favorite place to visit was Coronado Beach. As soon as we arrived, Basil became totally deaf to our calls and amused himself by running up and down like a wild man, challenging other dogs whenever he had the chance. He acted just like a kid turned loose on the sand, but unlike a child, he avoided the water since he despised getting wet.

We adopted a cat named Max and hoped that Basil and the kitty would get along with one another. At first Basil detested him, but suddenly, who knows why, they became great pals who ran and played together. Max would usually start a game of chase by teasing Basil, and then the race was on, with the cat outmaneuvering Basil most of the time. On one such occasion, Max leaped across our hot tub with feline agility, landing securely on the other side. Rambunctious Basil, who was in wild pursuit, was not so lucky. His legs fell short of the other side, and he ended up in the tub, humiliated and soaked to the skin, which he hated!

My husband and I often worked together on construction sites, and Basil usually came along with us. Just for fun, we frequently dressed him up and took pictures. One day we sat him on a chair in our office, wrapped a Levi jacket around him, and placed his left paw next to a coffee cup. His pose was hilarious, and we quickly grabbed the camera. It turned out to be one of my favorite pictures. I believe Basil found it as amusing as we did. In any event, he was surely a good sport.

Basil battled two episodes of a serious disorder caused by ticks. His health seemed to decline noticeably after the second bout, and toward the end of his life, he also developed anemia and kidney problems. Naturally, we hoped he would get better, and kept putting off the inevitable. When it finally became clear that his condition was hopeless, we decided that the kindest thing to do was to put him to sleep. We made a point of stopping by his favorite beach on the way to the vet, but Basil didn't even seem to know where he was. As we drove to the vet's office, we noticed a truck with a sign that read, "Jane's Transport." A few seconds later, Jane, our vet, called our cell phone to confirm Basil's appointment. The coincidence made the entire trip surreal.

Losing Basil was difficult for my husband and me. For days we conducted memorial services at home for him. We placed the urn of his ashes on the mantel above our fireplace and lit a candle. Often we put a vase of marigolds nearby, because these flowers are traditionally used by some cultures to honor the dead. We then reminisced about Basil, consoling each other over the loss of our beloved friend. The first week was especially hard. I had trouble sleeping, and when I was awake, I didn't want to do anything. I felt as if I were in a fog. The second week wasn't much better, until something remarkable happened.

I was standing by the kitchen sink, when without warning the windows began to rattle, as if a strong wind were blowing. Then I felt a presence in the room, and immediately thought of Basil. Goose bumps popped up all over my arms. Suddenly, I heard a loud buzzing noise close by me in the kitchen. I didn't have a clue what it was, but I began opening my kitchen cabinet doors to check inside. I found nothing. Then the sound led me to a drawer in the middle of the kitchen island. I opened the drawer and discovered that Basil's battery-powered clippers had turned on spontaneously! Somehow, the button had moved to the "On" position. I picked up the clippers and turned them off. It was really odd, because the clippers had been sitting silently in the drawer for a couple of months. They were new — I had used them only once on Basil before he died.

After I silenced the clippers, I began to associate the rattling of the windows with the feeling of a presence in the room and the phenomenon of that "On" button. I've never really been "into" paranormal experiences, but the timing of the incidents was remarkable. I believe that it could be possible that Basil somehow made it happen. Perhaps he was reaching out to let me know he was all right. But knowing Basil, he might also have been saying, "Thank God, she's not going to use those clippers on me again!" In any case, the incident has been a great comfort to me, although, of course, I continue to miss my special pal.

Harley *and* Lovey

…two elegant Briards, Harley and Lovey, whose lives were too short. They were lovingly cared for by Beth Schroeder, a librarian in Virginia whose hobby is dog training.

A fellow librarian told me about Briards, a relatively uncommon breed of dog. I was intrigued with his description, so as soon as a friend of mine had a litter of Briards, I went to look at them, and decided immediately to get one. When I first visited the pups, they were only four weeks old, and they all looked alike. Two weeks later they had developed differences in personality as well as in appearance so that now I could tell them apart. I carefully picked up and held each of the five youngsters. They were all so adorable I couldn't decide which one to choose. As I was standing there trying to make up my mind, I felt something on my foot. Looking down, I saw that one of the pups had fallen asleep on my shoe. Now I knew which one was mine.

Two weeks later, I took my new dog home and named him Harley. He grew up to have the most extraordinary, deep chestnut brown coat, one rarely seen in a Briard. Fully grown, he was a big dog, weighing 90 pounds. Despite his large size, he was friendly to everyone who came into our home, but because of his imposing appearance, other animals were often afraid of him. When my daughter's cat, "Pumpkin," first saw Harley, she reacted by arching her back, hissing, and making a terrible fuss. My gentle giant, on the other hand, only wanted to be friends. While the cat was carrying on like a soprano singing opera, Harley dropped down on the floor to make himself appear as small as possible, and then he wagged his tail to let Pumpkin know how loveable he was. It took the cat a minute or two to get the courage to investigate him, and when she did, Harley didn't move a muscle except for his tail, which was thumping happily. Once Pumpkin realized that "Harley the Ogre" would not hurt her, the two became buddies.

When Harley was six months old, I took him to an obedience training class. This was my first experience with obedience, and I absolutely loved it. I am quiet and shy by nature, and going to this class opened up a new world for me, a world of new friends and good times I could share with my dog. Harley loved it, too, and did well with the exercises necessary to complete the C.D. (Companion Dog) title. He even earned the coveted "High in Trial" trophy at a regional specialty show. Unfortunately, when he was three, his obedience career was cut short because of hip dysplasia. It was heartbreaking, but I was happy with what we had done together, and with the close, loving bond we shared. Still, I missed the camaraderie of the training classes and the excitement of the shows.

When Harley was four, I decided to get another Briard. She would be a companion for him as well as a dog I could train. Lovey was just four months old when she came into our lives. She bounded into the house and darted over to Harley, grabbing and pulling his hair. True to his gentle nature, Harley tolerated her youthful exuberance and accepted her as one of the family. The two of them quickly became best pals. Harley showed her how to chase squirrels, and in exchange, Lovey taught Harley how to play with toys. He had never been interested in them previously, but she soon had him playing tug of war. With some encouragement from me, Harley also learned to pick up a toy whenever the doorbell rang. With a bedraggled, fuzzy toy in his mouth, he was a far less intimidating giant to our guests!

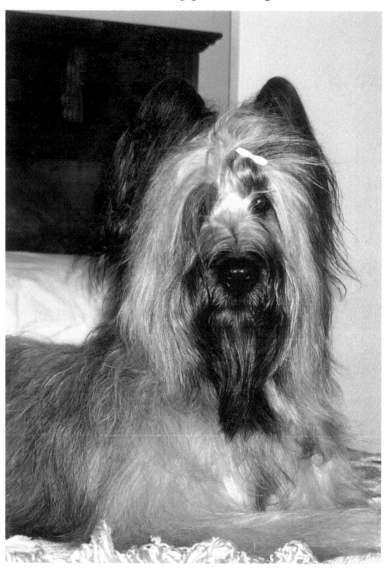

Lovey was a true beauty, smaller than Harley at just 70 pounds, and a beautiful platinum blonde who always wore a barrette in her hair. I called her my "Golden Girl." She, too, had a sweet disposition, but she was quite possessive of me and didn't like other dogs to get too close to me. I trained her in conformation, and she earned her championship quickly. Her wins were especially meaningful to me, as I always handled her myself — with limited funds, time, and experience. One of my fondest memories was showing her at the Westminster Kennel Club Show, a prestigious event open only to breed champions. That same year, Lovey was ranked as the eighth best Briard bitch in the country!

In addition to the recognition she received for being beautiful, Lovey enjoyed obedience training. By the time I started training her, the methods had changed from predominantly negative to positive motivational reinforcement. My training of Lovey was pure joy for both of us. She was attentive and consistent, and more energetic than Harley, and we quickly excelled in the sport. Retrieving the dumbbell was her favorite exercise. She won High in Trial at the National Briard Obedience Show, and one year, she was recognized as one of the country's top Briards in obedience. It was such a pleasure to show her, as I always felt as if we were one being in the ring. Lovey was a dream come true, and I couldn't have been happier. We were about to finish her CDX obedience title when our lives suddenly changed.

Three weeks after earning her High in Trial, Lovey woke up blind. I was in shock as I rushed her to the vet. Apparently, she had several tick-borne diseases that could have caused the blindness. Ticks are a problem where I live, and despite my keeping the dogs on Frontline and frequently examining them for ticks, Lovey managed to get infected. This unexpected turn of events upset all my plans for her future in obedience. For three weeks, I stayed home from work to care for her. Whenever I entered our training room and realized that I could never again do obedience with her, my left side began to ache and I felt truly ill. Lovey took it all in stride, however, and before long she was moving around the house with relative ease. Health problems continued to plague her, however, and shortly after the onset of blindness in December of 2000, she was diagnosed with lymphoma.

After careful deliberation, I decided to prolong her life with chemotherapy, especially because she was such a young dog, only four years old. For the first treatment, Lovey had to be away from me overnight. The night before her departure, I held her close and told her what would happen, and encouraged her not to be afraid. As I stroked her, she began to lick my face, and the licking went on for several minutes. She covered my face with "kisses," something she had never done before. I believe she was thanking me and telling me she would be all right. The next day my face was dry and scaly from the licking, but I didn't care. I would wear the "scabs" with pride as long as possible!

Lovey did quite well after her treatments, but to my dismay, a year later, Harley was also diagnosed with lymphoma. Then I had two dogs on chemo, and it was so expensive I had to get a home equity loan to pay

the bills! I never regretted my decision. I did everything I could to save my Briards, including putting them on special diets and making many trips to the vet.

Almost two years later, when it became apparent that Lovey was getting worse and was breathing rapidly, I knew it was time to euthanize her. I reassured her that she would go to heaven, and asked her to contact me to let me know she was all right. Her death was peaceful, and her snoring softly just before she passed away comforted me. I knew she was free of pain at last.

After Lovely was euthanized, I cried so much that going to work that day was impossible. I had meant to call a coworker at the library to ask her to take Lovey's picture off my desk, but I forgot. When I arrived at work the next day, I made a special effort not to look at the photo, but after the morning went by better than expected, I stole a quick glance. What I saw took my breath away. Her picture was glowing! The yellow frame around it was now bright gold. Emanating from it was

a soft but radiant light that was different from any I had ever seen! It brightened the entire corner of my office cubicle. As I became entranced with the light, the room became still. It was as if the whole world had stopped, and nothing existed except the brilliance radiating from Lovey's likeness. I suddenly felt peaceful and contented, something I had not felt for two years since Lovey's illness. After a while, the mystical glow began to fade, and grew less and less until it was entirely gone and the noise of the office returned.

I am a skeptical person, and I would not blame others for doubting my story. If it hadn't happened to me, I probably wouldn't believe it, either! But I have no doubt about what I saw. I know that somehow, Lovey was responsible for that light. It could not have come from an outside source, as there are no windows in my cubicle; it could not have been a reflection because the lights in my office are on continuously, and I have never seen that glow before or since that day. I had asked Lovey to contact me, and I truly believe she did.

That evening after work, I walked around my yard. I always keep it immaculate, and never allow bones or toys to be left outside. Imagine my surprise when I found, for the first and only time, one of Lovey's barrettes in my yard. I believe this was another sign to reassure me.

Afterward, I was alone with Harley, and I desperately wanted to keep him alive as long as possible. Every day after work we went for a walk with my friend Jan and her two rescued Greyhounds, Patti and Cyrano. Harley paid little attention to these dogs until one night as Jan and I stood talking, Harley went over and gently licked their faces. It was touching to see him behave in this unusual manner. I didn't think much about it at the time, but then I didn't know that Harley would be gone a month later. Looking back, I believe this was his way of saying goodbye to two old friends.

Just three months after Lovey died, Harley was hospitalized for the last time. He and I had just moved into our dream home. For days I had been encouraging him to be well enough to enjoy our new fireplace and chase the squirrels in his new backyard. I had been surprised at how rapidly he deteriorated, but I was thankful that he lasted longer than the vet predicted, just so we could share our new home together, even for a short time. Deciding to euthanize Harley was particularly difficult, because it followed Lovey's death so closely. When the day came, I was so distraught I didn't think to ask Harley to contact me when he got to heaven, as I had asked Lovey. My omission gnawed at me as I drove home, and I was sure I would not see or hear from him again.

As I pulled into my long driveway, I saw a squirrel between the two garage doors. The creature was exactly the same color as Harley — a deep, chestnut brown color, totally unlike the gray ones we always see in this area. I thought surely the squirrel would run away as I drove closer; instead, he sat up on his haunches and looked directly at me for a long time. Then he moved slowly into the woods behind my house. A feeling of relief and gratitude overwhelmed me, as I believe this was Harley's way of reassuring me and saying farewell.

After Harley died, a dear friend sent me a card with the following message:

"Perhaps they are not stars, but
rather openings in heaven where
the love of our lost ones
pours through and shines down upon us
to let us know they are happy."

This lovely quotation, inspired by an Eskimo legend, means so much to me. Every night as I lie in bed, I can see the stars through my bedroom window. Gazing at them, I say a prayer thanking God for giving me Harley and Lovey, and for allowing them to send me assurance of their well-being in the afterlife.

" You think that these dogs will not be in Heaven! I tell you
they will be there long before any of us."

… Robert Louis Stevenson

Herbie

...a Miniature Poodle from California who lived for about 12 years with dog trainer Shirley Indelicato.

The new arrival was a Miniature Poodle. He was a chocolate-colored breed champion, just over a year old, and he had that "look-at-me" attitude. He was brought to me in the hope of being adopted, because he did not get along well with the other dog in his family. As soon as I saw him walking into my house, I cried. I loved him immediately. My husband, on the other hand, did not want to keep him, but my daughter and I insisted, and Herbie got to stay.

I started training Herbie in obedience as soon as I could. He was just the dog I had been waiting for — beautiful and energetic, with a "Hot Shot" personality. Although he learned quickly, he was a show-off and often found a better way to do the exercises. Once, at a trial in Mexico, Herbie decided to do all the exercises his way. Instead of one drop in the recall exercise, he did two. When it was time for the dumbbell retrieve, he managed to go over the jump an extra time and then deliver the dumbbell to the judge, instead of to me! I was mortified. He finished off his performance by leaping over the broad jump two times rather than doing it the way he should, only once. The spectators went wild, yelling and screaming throughout his performance. The audience loved Herbie so much they wanted to know when I was going to show him again. They couldn't wait for an encore!

Herbie had a trademark behavior. If he liked you, he would poke his cold, wet nose into your arm or leg, hoping that you would pay attention to him. His poking was usually reserved for people, although he would occasionally nudge a Golden Retriever. To my knowledge, he never poked any other breed of dog.

Despite his antics and clownish behavior from time to time, Herbie did well in obedience, and by the time he was 12, he needed only ten more points to earn his OTCH (Obedience Trial Championship). Unfortunately, he was not able to finish his title because of a horrible accident. A male Weimaraner, whom we were temporarily keeping at the house, leapt through a glass window and attacked Herbie. The sudden violence was probably incited by the presence of a bitch in season. The Weimaraner's attack was vicious, crushing and breaking many of Herbie's ribs, and causing extensive injuries to his lungs. We rushed Herbie to the vet immediately, but nothing could be done to save him. It broke my heart to have him put down, and in addition, I felt extremely guilty about the accident.

The next day, my daughter and I, both upset about Herbie's death, sat at the dinner table and had little to say to each other. With no dogs and no other people around, the house was unusually quiet. About halfway through the meal, I suddenly and distinctly felt a cold, wet nose poke my leg twice. Startled and a bit frightened, I looked up at my daughter and exclaimed, "I just got poked twice on my leg!"

My daughter got a funny look on her face and replied, "Oh, Mom! I did, too!"

We finished dinner in silence, feeling apprehensive and speechless about what had happened to us. The shock of it returned each time I thought about the incident. I told a few friends what had happened, and one of them assured me that Herbie had simply returned to greet us and let us know that he was all right. From that time on, I was able to feel more comfortable and less guilty about Herbie's death.

Although many years have passed, I still miss my "Hot Shot" boy. Herbie was cremated and his ashes were placed in a special wooden trophy box in our family room. His name is on the box, along with the titles he earned in breed and obedience. I still see in my mind's eye my beautiful chocolate clown putting on a show for the spectators at the obedience trials and enchanting the judges with his "look at me!" attitude.

Dakota

...a German Shepherd dog, who for his brief three years of life, was dear to the heart of Kari Selinger, a certified athletic trainer, obedience and agility instructor who lives in Michigan.

Sometimes a name comes to us years before we meet its owner. Ever since I was a young girl, I had loved the name "Dakota." All I needed was a special dog worthy of my favorite name. One day, my fiancé bought a German Shepherd puppy as a wedding gift for me, and I knew I had found my special dog. Dakota was ten weeks old when he came to live with us. He was a confident and playful little dog, who had the biggest ears I have ever seen! He reminded me of the cartoon dog, Pluto, which would have been a good name for him had I not already decided on Dakota. Even after he matured, he did not outgrow those ears!

We lived in a small apartment when he came to us, but that didn't stop Dakota from growing. Bigger and bigger he grew, until he equaled the length of our bathtub when measured from the tail to the nose! Dakota weighed 95 pounds. He wasn't fat, just tall, long, and lanky!

Dakota had a tremendous spirit, always sensitive, always willing to please, and always trying hard not to make a mistake. I never needed to use food as a motivator when I trained him. All it took was a loving pat on his head, followed by a genuine "Good boy." He liked most toys, but Dakota's greatest passion was chasing a tennis ball! We played fetch with it often after a training session, and he never wanted to quit.

By the time he was just *three* years old, Dakota had earned several titles: one in tracking, two in novice agility, and most impressive, a C.D., a C.D.X. (Companion Dog and Companion Dog Excellent), and two legs toward his Utility Degree in Obedience. It is necessary to earn three "legs" under three different judges before one attains each title; one earns a leg if the dog completes the course successfully.

German Shepherds, like many of the larger breeds, are not the easiest to train in obedience, but we were well on our way to the U.D. If you have ever trained or shown a dog, you will realize what a remarkable accomplishment this all was for such a young dog. Dakota was absolutely a dream come true, and I couldn't have been happier.

One Sunday as we were competing for our last Utility leg, Dakota's behavior suddenly changed. Between exercises, as the judge moved close to us, Dakota's eyes appeared to cross, and he turned quickly and nipped the judge. Afterward, he returned to me and acted as if nothing had happened. I knew that something was terribly wrong, as this was so contrary to his gentle disposition. I apologized profusely to the judge, who, of course, excused us from the ring.

The following day, I took Dakota to the vet, who discovered that he had a brain tumor. I was stunned! My beautiful Dakota was only *three* years old! My husband and I decided to have the vet treat the tumor, but the regimen he used proved ineffective. The quality of Dakota's life deteriorated rapidly, and less than three months later, we knew it was time to euthanize him – especially when he no longer showed any interest in his tennis ball.

The day Dakota was going to be euthanized, my husband and I both stayed with him, having planned to do some of the special things our dog enjoyed most. Unfortunately, he was unable to do much because of his illness, but he was happy just to be with us, and, of course, we kept his tennis ball nearby. Our last stop was the veterinary clinic, where my husband and I let Dakota lie across our laps as he passed from this world to the next.

Just as Dakota died, I was astonished to see something white rise from his body. It is hard to put into words, but this something was circular, opaque, and pure white. It appeared brighter in the middle and faded along the sides. I felt as if I were looking at a sea of white that extended forever. I remember thinking, "That must be Dakota's soul!"

Then, as my husband and I were leaving the vet's office, I saw Dakota right in front of me! It was as if he were standing on his hind legs, with his front paws on my shoulders. He looked directly at me for a second or two, panting and happy. He appeared solid and real in every way! Although my husband didn't see Dakota, he told me later that he had sensed his presence very strongly as I was experiencing this encounter.

It is unusual for me to remember even pleasant dreams, but I had two vivid and unforgettable ones about Dakota during the first week after his death. One dream was filled with fond memories of all the things we used to enjoy together; in the other, Dakota was still alive and active, being a natural part of our current "pack" of dogs. In addition to the dreams, one time as I was sitting in the kitchen, I had the sensation of Dakota's presence and felt him lay his head in my lap.

There were no further contacts with Dakota until more than a year later. Then, on at least five different occasions, I sensed Dakota by my side, and saw him out of the corner of my eye. If I turned to look or to touch him or to pat his head, he would disappear. These visits happened at home, usually in the early evening, as I went about my daily routine. Dakota had always loved to follow me around the house, and these quick visions occurred as I moved from room to room. Although there were no other human beings present when I had these experiences, I had other dogs and cats with me, and I'm certain that at least two of my pets were aware of Dakota's presence. One was my cat, Kismet, who was close to Dakota and had always loved to play with him. She loved to rub against him and bat his head with her little paw as if she were petting him. When I saw Dakota out of the corner of my eye, Kismet was sitting at attention, purring and focusing her gaze directly on the spot where I had seen the vision seconds earlier!

Another incident proved especially powerful in convincing me that Dakota was still with us. It involved my female German Shepherd, Mischief, who had known Dakota. A split second after I felt Dakota's presence and saw a fleeting image of him, Mischief began to whimper and prance around as she used to when she greeted Dakota! It was obvious that Mischief could either see Dakota or that she was aware of him in some other way.

About 18 months after Dakota's death, we were considering adding another German Shepherd to our little "pack." A friend of mine had a promising litter and offered me a puppy, but my husband and I weren't sure we were ready. While we were deciding what to do, I began to sense Dakota's presence again. My "visitations" from Dakota were so positive that I felt reassured it would be all right – we had Dakota's approval to bring a new puppy into our life.

I have described the encounters with Dakota without in any way excusing or denying them, but I must admit that I have been a bit skeptical at times. I've wondered if the visions and experiences were just my imagination, just a way for me to deal with my emotions. Having said that, I immediately sense a conflict, because I truly do believe that my contacts with Dakota have served to validate my belief that animals have a soul and an afterlife.

Sunny

...a happy little red-haired mixture of Keeshond and Corgi who made Siouxsan Eisen's life exciting for 16 years. She is a dog trainer who now lives in Missouri.

When my parents finally yielded to my persistent begging for a dog, I was ten years old. By then they deemed me old enough and sufficiently responsible to take care of a pet, and I practically dragged them to the pound. My dream was to own a purebred Corgi, but that was beyond our financial means. As destiny would have it, there was a young Corgi mix up for adoption who had been found wandering alongside of a road. He looked like a little fox, and was the cutest thing I had ever seen. He was mine from the moment we met, and I named him Sunny because of his cheerful disposition. I remember sitting in the hallway when we brought him home, petting him and thinking, "I'm going to love him forever!"

Sunny would jump on my chest every morning to wake me up, his tail thumping with excitement while he uttered a soft "grumbling" noise. This mumbling was a special greeting reserved only for me. I never heard him vocalize his joy in that way for anyone else. As I hugged him and fussed over him, he mumbled louder and louder, letting me know how much he enjoyed the attention. Saturday was my favorite day because Sunny and I spent all day together. I packed a lunch and water, and the two of us went for a long hike across the sparsely populated areas of Santa Rosa, California. Sunny stayed close to me unless he was chasing butterflies. Then off he'd go, bounding over the grass, his short legs gathering momentum as he prepared to leap into the air. My little fox never caught a butterfly, but that never stopped him from trying.

Although I have had other pets since then, it was Sunny who was the most significant dog in my life. As a young girl I was very shy, and Sunny being so cute encouraged other people to be friendly and talk to me. As I grew up, Sunny was with me through every major event in my life. He was there to comfort me when my father died, tragically and too young. He was there when I got married at 19. He was there for the birth of my daughter, and for my divorce several months later, and during the sadness that always follows when a marriage fails.

While I was going through my divorce, I thought it would be best for Sunny to live with my mother for a short time. She needed my happy little red-haired dog to comfort her as she adjusted to my father's death. This temporary arrangement would also give me time to find a job so that I could support my daughter. When the time came for Sunny to return to my house, I'll never forget that crucial discussion with my mother. At first she said, "I would really hate for you to move Sunny. He's eleven now. It's going to be hard for him to adjust to a new home." When I persisted, my mother finally confessed, "I need him!" That ended the conversation, and Sunny continued to live with my mother, in the home I grew up in.

When Sunny reached the age of 16, he seemed to be in good health, but he was obviously slowing down. Then one day, I had an upsetting phone call from my mother. Sunny had stopped eating and drinking. All he wanted to do was lie in his favorite spot, even though he could still walk. Mother took him to the vet, who assured her that Sunny was not suffering, but that he was ready to go. It was just a matter of time.

When I went to visit him, despite his weakened state, his eyes still lit up and that long tail of his slowly thumped on the ground. Though somewhat feebly, he still growled and grumbled as he had always done to greet me. I stayed with him all that day and through the night. He slept next to me in the crook of my arm, just like my childhood days, before my father died and my marriage failed. After a tearful hug, I left the next morning to return to my home.

The next night, a rather persistent knocking at my front door awakened me. It was just past two o'clock. "Who on earth could be knocking at my door at this hour," I wondered. I sensed that an elderly gentleman was outside, possibly needing help and pleading for attention. Without hesitation, I ran to open the door. There was no one there! Suddenly I wondered why I had opened the door for a stranger. It was so unlike me! Then followed the unmistakable sensation that *someone* was inside my house. Feeling eerie and nervous, I looked everywhere, going through all the closets, checking behind the shower curtain, *even* looking up at the ceilings. I couldn't find anyone. Finally, I went back to bed, but I found it impossible to sleep. I kept wondering why I, "Miss Cautious," had opened the door and why I could still sense the presence of someone in my house.

At five, the phone rang. It was my mother, in tears. She told me that Sunny had died peacefully in his sleep a few hours earlier...around two, she thought. I suddenly realized that the presence I had been feeling was not an elderly gentleman, but Sunny! Apparently, he had visited me before crossing the Rainbow Bridge. It was this precious gift that helped me cope with losing my first dog.

That was not the end of his visits, though. Years later, I finally felt ready to get another dog, even though the memory of Sunny still lingered in my mind. Eventually I found my new pup, a little red Sheltie I named Dusty. As I brought him home, I wondered if I would ever love him as much as I had loved Sunny. Dusty was with me only a short time when Sunny visited me in a powerful dream. In it, I went back home to visit my mother. She appeared to be much younger, and was wearing her hair long again, swept up in a bun, just as she did when I was growing up. Glowing with happiness, my mother told me she had a big surprise for me. She took me to my bedroom, which was decorated just as it had been when I was a child. Suddenly, running down the hallway, barking, grumbling, and talking, came my beloved Sunny. "Sunny!" I yelled, as he leapt into my arms. I could feel his weight and smell his little doggy smell. Best of all, I could touch him again and run my hands through his rough fur. My joy was so profound I moaned loudly and woke myself up!

The dream with Sunny was so real that he had to have been there with me! I felt sad momentarily because now that I was awake, Sunny was gone. Then I looked down and was reassured that Sunny had contacted me. There, nestled in the crook of my arm, in the very spot where Sunny used to sleep, lay my new puppy. Leave it to my dog on the "Other Side" to erase any of my doubts about my new pup on this side!

Foxy

...an independent little "runaway dog," who at the age of six, ran straight into the hearts of Bill Mason and his wife, Sudie, and stayed there for 12 years. Foxy was probably a Sheltie-Pomeranian mix, but he didn't bring his pedigree with him when he found the Masons. They live in the state of Washington and their hobby is boating.

Foxy has no tombstone that future generations can stand before. Only a barely discernible hump remains in our backyard lawn, and this will vanish in time. His story must be told so that people will know that he was a cherished member of our family, a prize among canines, and that he returned after his death to let me know he was safe and well.

It was April 1984 when I first saw him. My boat, a 34-foot cabin cruiser, was moored in the east boat haven at Port Angeles, Washington. I was frequently down on the docks, and one day this little reddish-brown and tan dog came racing to greet me. He barked happily, as if he knew me, and jumped over and over again, almost as high as my head, to say "Hello!" I talked to him, petted him, and then went about my business. Every day for about a week he greeted me in the same way. No one seemed to know anything about the little guy. I quickly became very fond of him and asked my wife, Sudie, if she would like to adopt a dog. She agreed with some reluctance since we had an old cat, "Baby Kitty," at home. I looked forward to picking up my wayward friend the next day, but I could not find him. I hunted everywhere along the docks, but to no avail. After searching for several days, I came to the conclusion that his owner had claimed him, or that someone had adopted him. I confess I felt a sense of loss. He was such a personable little dog.

Since Sudie and I had decided to adopt a dog, I swung by the Humane Society to see what dogs were available. The attendant took me to the kennel area, and the first dog I saw was my boat haven friend! He was so excited to see me that I have no doubt he recognized me. The attendant warned me about adopting him. "This dog is a runaway. Turn your back for thirty seconds and he will be gone. He has been in and out of this shelter for the last three years. You can find a much better dog than this one." These words of warning fell on deaf ears. Minutes later, I walked out of the building with my friend.

On the way home, we stopped at the vet's. The vet estimated that my dog was about six, and was probably a Sheltie-Pomeranian mix. I named him "Foxy" because his little face looked like a fox's. He had some afflictions, including a severe underbite that made him look as if he were smiling all the time, an enlarged heart that was pressing against his esophagus, causing him to choke occasionally, a heart murmur, and a million fleas. After he got his shots and a dog tag, I took him home.

The next order of business was to give him a flea bath. He didn't care much for the bath, but he stood still and tolerated what had to be done. Afterward, we settled down in the dining room with a towel, brush, comb, and hair dryer. When the job was finished, he was the fluffiest, cleanest, softest ball of fuzz you could ever imagine. This prompted one of several nicknames, "Fuzz Face." Then we introduced Foxy to "Baby Kitty." Our cat was hardly a baby, as he was eight years old, but his original name stuck. During the day, the two animals were quiet and coexisted peacefully, but after we went to bed, we heard them racing and tearing through the house like a herd of wildebeests. It was never clear who was chasing whom, and there never appeared to be a declared winner of whatever contest they had indulged in. Apparently a truce was declared after a few weeks as our home returned to being peaceful and quiet at night.

Foxy had runaway problems, just as the Humane Society employee had warned. Several times when I looked away for a moment, he was gone. He always wore a collar with his name and phone number, making it possible for me to retrieve him from someone's house or business within a few hours. Luckily for us, he managed to stay clear of the dogcatcher. I remember one day in particular when he ran off, I got a call from a large downtown motel. Foxy was following the maids from room to room, seeking attention and a friendly pat on the head. In less than an hour, he had traveled downtown and at least two miles across the area to the motel!

In the fall of 1985, Baby Kitty died of leukemia, and then Foxy was our only pet. I took him for two long walks every day. Early in the morning, we hiked in a semi-rural area of trees, brush, and dirt roads; around noon, we walked over two miles through the residential districts. At first I was wary about letting him off leash, but I soon realized that he had been trained to obey certain commands, including "sit," "stay," "come here," and "NO!" Once I discovered that I could control him, I took the leash off to let him roam freely. The only problem was cats. If I saw the cat first, I had to start talking to Foxy right away. "Heel now! Right here. Be good. Heel. No, you're not going to chase that cat!" He'd be a good boy and we would walk right past that cat, but all the time his eyes would be rolling out of his head! If he saw the cat first, though, he would take one running jump and the chase was on. Then I had no way of stopping him. One day I was washing my truck in the alley and watching to be sure that the little guy didn't take off to explore the world. All of a sudden, he bolted. I yelled, but to no avail. Two houses down the alley, I saw the neighbors' cat, sleeping in the driveway. He was a curled-up ball of fur, enjoying the sunshine and completely oblivious of Foxy bearing down on him. Foxy was running so fast that he was a blur as he approached the cat that didn't move. Suddenly you could sense his thought: "Hey! You're supposed to run! What's the matter with you?" At the last moment, Foxy tried to stop, but it was too late. The cat woke up and, in a panic, jumped to the side. Unfortunately it was to the wrong side, and the two animals collided and rolled over and over down the alley. Foxy finally picked himself up and watched as the terrified cat scampered away. Neither of them was hurt.

As far as other dogs were concerned, Foxy was interested only in larger breeds, especially Great Danes and black Labs. He shunned smaller ones with disdain. Several times he got too friendly with a large dog, and a scuffle ensued. Foxy was no coward, and he never ran or tried to hide behind me. He fought with startling ferocity. Even in his later years, when all his teeth were gone, he fought with his gums snapping and his lips snarling. When he was 13, he ran to greet a black Lab on the boating dock. The Lab snapped at him, as if to declare, "What do you think you're doing, Shorty? Who do you think you are?" Foxy held his ground and began to bark. With his toothless gums bared, he hurled himself at the Lab, who backed away quickly. Foxy was never hurt in these exchanges. The larger animal probably felt ashamed for fighting with such a little guy, who, after all, weighed only about 17 pounds.

Every summer, from June to mid-August, we took our 34-foot cruiser north to the sparsely populated areas of British Columbia. Several of our grandchildren as well as some adult guests usually accompanied us. Foxy loved these trips, except when he got seasick as we crossed the rough waters of the Juan de Fuca or Georgia Straits, and he had to take tranquilizers. Once we were anchored, he was ready for a ride in our dinghies or in the kayak. He was always so excited that it was almost impossible not to take him. Sudie took him in her kayak whenever she could, and he would sit happily in her lap, watching the marine landscape pass by. If Sudie went without him, Foxy would stand by the rail of our cruiser and watch as long as she was in sight. By looking at Foxy, you could always tell where Sudie was.

We went ashore frequently to hike or to dig for clams and oysters. Our little "Fuzz Face" loved these excursions and ran like a maniac along the shore, or searched for chipmunks in the rocky cliffs. On the days that we didn't go hiking, we put Foxy ashore to get some exercise, while we paddled along close to him. He followed us, climbing from rock to rock along the beach. Afterward, we pulled up onto the beach and he jumped into the dinghy.

He never enjoyed swimming, and it was just as well, because his thick hair was quickly waterlogged and weighed him down, putting him in danger of drowning. One evening, Sudie and my grandson Christopher took Foxy ashore for his constitutional. Foxy jumped out onto the beach, expecting young Chris to follow him. Instead, Sudie rowed back out into the bay with Chris. Foxy became very upset and plunged into the ocean to swim toward the departing dinghy. We had noticed that Foxy was frequently jealous of our grandchildren, as he always wanted to be the center of attention. Apparently he could not bear to see Chris alone with "his" mother. Of course Sudie and Chris rescued the soggy, jealous little guy.

Foxy loved to play with an old flannel baby sheet, which was his security blanket. Every night he pawed at it, tossed it into the air, and uttered an unusual vocalization, a combination of moaning, mumbling, growling, and barking. We called this sound "garwoofing." He acted as though he was trying to arrange the blanket as a sleeping pad. Sometimes he even tried to wear his blanket, and grumbled when it did not fit. He rarely slept on it when we were on land, but on the cruiser he cuddled up to it almost every night.

At home, Foxy had another favorite routine, which also involved "garwoofing." At bedtime he would jump up on our high, antique bed and position himself just below the pillows. Sliding both paws over and under the top edge of the bedspread, he turned our covers down with a mighty heave. Then he dived below the pillows, tossed them into the air, and dug at the covers until he had everything rearranged to his liking. In the mayhem, the pillows often ended up on the floor, but it was such a joy seeing him having so much fun that we did not care. In later years, when arthritis prevented him from jumping, we would help him onto the bed. His antics were slower and less exuberant, but there he was, every night, helping to make our bed more comfortable. After he finished his "garwoofing," we would help him down. In all the years we had him, he never stayed to sleep with us. His domain was beside or under the bed.

Toward the end of his life, Foxy's body began to deteriorate, and he was a mere shadow of the dog we first adopted. He lived for his summers on the boat, but during his 18th year, there was a distinct change in him. As soon as we came home, he seemed to give up, and we knew it was time to say goodbye. We called the vet, who came to our house at noon to administer the injection. Afterward we wrapped him in his security blanket and buried him in the backyard.

My wife and I felt intense grief that never seemed to end. We had decided there would be no more pets after Baby Kitty and Foxy, but as our mourning continued, we thought a new dog might help us heal and bring us peace. After three emotionally troubling months, we adopted a baby Sheltie and named him Edward. Our new dog reminded us a lot of Foxy, but having him did not seem to assuage our grief. Little Edward was starting his training, learning to sit, stay, heel, and come. Every day I took him for walks, just as I had done with Foxy. I frequently sensed that Foxy was still with me, and feeling jealous as he watched me with the puppy.

One foggy morning, Edward and I stepped out to begin our morning walk. My house sits about 50 feet from the street and is probably ten feet below street level, so that you need to look slightly upward to see the pavement. As I left the house and walked toward the driveway, I happened to glance up at the street. I froze. There was Foxy! He was standing still, and looking straight ahead. A thin rope leash stretched upward at a slight angle from his collar and vanished high above in the early morning mist. I wondered what or who was holding his leash. While I stood motionless, staring at my old friend, Foxy turned his head and looked briefly at me, as if to say, "I'm going for a walk, too!" Then he looked straight ahead and did not glance back at me.

Several seconds later, he slowly disappeared, seemingly swallowed by a fine mist that was unlike the morning fog. I never saw him leave the ground or move away. He just slowly vanished.

After he disappeared, I went on with my walk, my day, and my life. My deep grief was gone. Now I knew Foxy still existed, that he was being cared for and that he was going for walks, too. Seeing him that morning comforted me in a way that no other experience could have. Now I have no doubt that I will see him again when I make my trip across the "Rainbow Bridge."

Gus

...a blue merle Collie who lived happily for 13 years with Lenore Tirgrath, a dog groomer, trainer, and mom.

It is strange how you keep things to yourself, wondering how people will react if you tell them about an extraordinary experience. Then along comes this book, and for some reason, I am willing to tell my story now. I hope that what I have to say will help people realize that their deceased pets are still around them. Now in spirit form, they are immortal. I believe the love between pets and their owners lasts forever.

Dogs have always been a part of my life. My preference for the last 16 years has been blue merle Collies, stemming from the absolutely fabulous relationship I had with my first one, Gus. I was not familiar with the coloring of the blues until I saw them in the Collie ring at a show. Someone has described blue merles as being the color of "blueberries floating in cream." Some of the berries have been gently bruised and have turned the cream to a powdery blue; others are still whole, and give the illusion of being black as they float in cream that is white and sparkling. The colors have been splashed onto the dog as if by a giant paintbrush, and there are no two alike! I thought they were the most beautiful dogs I had ever seen. One owner gave me his card and told me he had nothing available then, but might have in a few months. Fourteen months later, he called to say he had a pup for sale. At the time, I was pregnant with my son, Richie, and was not interested in adding a puppy to the family, but the man was insistent. "Just come and take a look," he said.

My husband, daughter, and I got into the car and drove 45 minutes to see a puppy that we never intended to buy. When we arrived, I spotted him immediately. He was a roly-poly little guy, just seven weeks old. Our eyes met. I picked him up, and instantly fell in love. From that moment until we got home, I didn't let him out of my arms, and he was content to be there. We decided to name him "Gus," and he was such a bright, well-mannered puppy. He was housebroken in just four days, and he had the freedom of the entire house. If he did have an accident, he would always go to the farthest corner of the basement.

At seven weeks, Gus weighed only five pounds, but he grew to be a 75-pound adult, a good size for the breed. He was gentle and tolerant, never showing aggression toward people or other animals. He even tolerated Baby Richie, who grabbed him and pulled his hair and ran his small toys over him. After enduring Richie's shenanigans, Gus would come to me and look into my eyes, as if to say, "Can you believe what Richie just did to me?"

Gus was about four years old when I adopted a crippled baby Blue Jay. I nursed him back to health in six months. "Blue" could hop around, but he never learned to fly. He loved to walk all over the big Collie, and sometimes he even made a little nest in Gus's hair and slept there. Gentle Gus didn't mind at all. Blue lived happily with our family for 13 years.

One of Gus's most endearing traits was his constant focus on me. Even if I was in a crowd, or busy talking to someone, he never took his eyes off me. Many people told me they had never seen such devotion. Despite our close attachment, Gus was never a nuisance, preferring to communicate his love by watching me and looking into my eyes. Each of us seemed to know what the other was thinking. Many times when I was reading, sitting at my desk, or puttering about the kitchen, I would suddenly think about going for a walk. At the same time, Gus would lift his head, stare at me for a few seconds, and then get up and jump around excitedly, waiting for me to get his leash and collar. This happened repeatedly, at different times of the day and under various circumstances. Perhaps he was picking up subtle body clues from me, but I am convinced that he was reading my mind!

Our special closeness prompted me to train and show Gus in obedience trials. Although I had trained dogs before, Gus was my first competition dog, and I trained him in a most untraditional manner all the way through his Utility Dog degree. It was more like thinking and mentally projecting what I wanted him to do. He responded as though he understood my thoughts, and true to his character, he learned the exercises in no time. So much of our relationship was that way. Our souls, not our voices, talked to each other. In the silent moments when we were together, there was such communication, always reminding me of our special bond.

Our connection was made stronger because we shared so many activities. Besides doing obedience, Gus and I performed in demonstrations for children with special needs, and marched together in many parades. Gus even became the town's mascot! He played "Sandy" in the musical *Annie*, even though an Airedale was usually cast in the part. The script just called for "a large, hairy dog," and Gus fit the description so well he earned the role three times.

When Gus was nine, I purchased another blue merle Collie, whom we named Gus's Goodfella. We called him "Fella," and I was able to complete his Utility Dog title, not long after Gus died. The dogs played together and got along well, but they never seemed to be close buddies.

Toward the end of his life, Gus was neurologically impaired. It was never determined whether he suffered from vertigo or from some nameless malady, but the condition prevented him from walking properly. I had to help him up, and he would stagger across the room, leaning against walls or cabinets for support. Gus always leaned on his right side. When there was nothing to lean against, he would accelerate his pace to get to the next thing that would support him. In the house, his final destination was always a favorite rug in the living room. Once there, he would literally collapse, and be content to stay for hours. Although his condition wasn't painful, it was debilitating and growing worse. The vet advised me to put him down, but I just couldn't make that decision, even though it was difficult to see him so handicapped.

After he had been ill for about a month, I sat with him one evening and cried. I begged him softly, "Please take the decision away from me and go where you have to go right now. Please don't make me end your life." Gus lifted his head and looked at me intently for about ten seconds. Strangely enough, he had an excited, happy expression. Even though he hadn't eaten for several days, I offered him some food, and he ate it. A surge of hope swept over me. "Maybe the vet is wrong, and Gus will get better," I thought. For days, I had slept by Gus, but that night, believing he might be getting better, I stayed with him only a few hours and then went to my room to sleep. Not long afterward, I awoke with a start and ran downstairs. Gus was unconscious, and within an hour he passed away peacefully. Was it merely a coincidence? In my heart, I believe that he understood what I had said, and loved me enough to die on his own, the very night I asked him to go!

The morning Gus crossed over, my entire family was in the depths of grief. Even four-year-old Fella grieved, which surprised me. He kept pawing at Gus's dead body and doing play-bows. When there was no response, he would look dejected and lay his head on the dead body for a while. Whimpering softly, Fella would look at me, then at Gus, and then walk out of the room, only to return and repeat his mourning ritual. Fella continued his vigil until I took him outside so he wouldn't see my husband removing Gus's body for cremation. Fella rested on the grass for about ten minutes and then came over to the bottom of the steps. I looked down at him and thought I must be seeing things. He had the same expression Gus always had when he wanted me to open the door. I had never thought the dogs looked much alike.

What happened next was so shocking I thought surely I must be dreaming. Fella staggered up the three steps, and at the top, he leaned on his right side against the house. He increased his pace as I opened the door, and he moved across the kitchen to the cabinets, remaining propped up exactly the way Gus had done it to avoid falling. Continuing on his way, he staggered across the kitchen and leaned against the stove, against more cabinets, and then against the pantry doors. When Fella reached the open space into the living room, he copied Gus exactly by accelerating his pace and then plopping down on the same rug where Gus used to lie. I was stunned! Fella's movements so flawlessly mirrored Gus's ritual, I might as well have been looking at Gus himself!

Twelve-year-old Richie was with me at the time, witnessing everything that happened. Without any prompting from me, my son commented, "I think that was Gus's way of telling us that he's always going to be with us." I was in disbelief at what I had seen, but Richie's words reassured me that the events really had taken place. I immediately understood what my son had said. "Yes," I replied, "Gus left our home this morning through the front door, and returned through the back door inside Fella!"

Worried that Fella might have the same disease as Gus, I took him to the vet shortly after the incident. We were delighted to discover that our dog was healthy, with no evidence of any neurological disorder. When I told the vet what I had observed, he completely discounted my story, dismissing it as "simply a manifestation of grief." Saying it was just grief makes no sense to me! How could grief make a healthy dog mimic precisely a long sequence of behaviors that he had never seen? Because Gus had difficulty maintaining his balance, I *never* allowed Fella to accompany us whenever I took Gus into the house or into the backyard. Fella could join us once we were situated. Before that day, Fella had never exhibited any staggering or leaning, nor has he since, now over three years ago! The only explanation that makes any sense is Richie's assertion that Gus came back to let us know that he will always be with us. I believe the spirit of Gus temporarily entered Fella's body and made him repeat actions that he had never seen!

Gus was cremated and his ashes placed in a lovely urn, which I have on my nightstand. His picture is always with me. One picture is next to my bed, one is in my car, and another is in my wallet. Although I keep these constant reminders, I really do not need them to remember my beloved blue merle Collie, Scotwarrior Duke Of Dennison, U.D. – or just plain "Gus."

Scruffy

...a Brittany/Aussie mix who lived for 15 years with his best friend, a woman who is a teacher in California.

Scruffy, my first dog, visited me within an hour after he died! At most, I had hoped to see his image in a dream, or perhaps sense his presence, but I had never imagined that he would return so that I could actually hear him!

I was 22 and single when Scruffy came unexpectedly into my life. Some boys brought him into the youth center where I was working, and although I was not looking for a dog, I fell in love with him immediately. He was a brown and white mix of Brittany and Aussie, about five months old, very affectionate and full of energy. I agreed to take him for a few days while the boys found him a home. A few days turned into a lifetime, with Scruffy becoming my constant companion and best friend.

Scruffy loved to run, and his favorite place was the beach, where I took him often. It was uncanny how he always knew we were going there. He would jump eagerly into the car and sit in his favorite place beside me on the front seat. Once the car was moving, he would stick his head out the window and become "the flying dog," with his long ears flopping in the wind and the hair fanning out on the sides of his head. As soon as we arrived at the beach, he leapt out of the car with great joy and excitement to begin his ritual of running, barking, and chasing birds along the shore, while avoiding the water because he did not like to get wet. I  usually brought a ball along so we could play "retrieve," but if I forgot it, Scruffy was satisfied to chase just about anything I could find on the beach. He often initiated a game of retrieve by bringing me a stick to throw.

The "stick" might be three or four times the length of his body, and he could hardly drag it across the sand, but that never deterred him from trying. I was reminded of James Thurber's story of his Bull Terrier, Rex, who once tried to drag a chest of drawers up the front steps of their home! I don't think Scruffy would have gone that far, but he was always exhausted from running, chasing, barking, and dragging by the time we were ready to leave. As I drove home, my flying dog became my sleeping dog, stretched out on the backseat.

Scruffy lived a long, happy, active life for many years. He began to slow down gradually as he aged, and by the time he was 15, he was too weak to run. When that ability was gone, the quality of his life was compromised, and he was not a happy dog. Although I did not want to let him go, I realized that euthanasia was the kindest and most loving thing I could do for him. The day before his appointment, I took him to the beach for the last time, but he was almost too weak to walk.

The next morning as I drove to the vet, Scruffy laid his head on my lap. I sang to him, just as I had often done, so that he would not think anything was wrong. At the same time, I was trying to reassure myself that Scruffy and I would always be together in spirit. I asked him to visit me to let me know that our bond would never be broken. Scruffy passed away peacefully, and I left his body with the vet for cremation.

Words cannot describe the loneliness I felt as I drove home. I had lost my first dog, a dog who had been the joy of my life for 15 years. Scruffy was all I could think about as I arrived home in tears. When I entered my house and walked into the living room, I noticed how quiet it was. Minutes passed. Suddenly I heard the clicking of nails and the pitter-patter of footsteps on my kitchen floor. I stood motionless, shocked by what I had heard. My kitchen is just a few feet from the living room, and I distinctly heard seven or eight footsteps, which sounded exactly like Scruffy crossing the floor! An eerie feeling came over me. "Scruffy?" I called hesitantly, wondering if I had imagined hearing him. Then I heard the footsteps again! This time I was sure that it was not just my imagination. I went into the kitchen to look for him. Although I never saw or heard him again, I knew he had been in the house, and that he had responded to my wish to return to me. "Thank you, Scruffy, for letting me know you are okay," I whispered. I was certain that he would be looking down on me for the rest of my life.

After receiving Scruffy's cremated remains, I scattered a portion of the ashes at home and some at the beach where we had played so often. The rest I kept with me, along with some of his hair. Many times I have thought about my afterlife encounter with Scruffy. I had always believed that animals have souls and that they exist after death. Now I know that it is true.

Spooky

...a Terrier-Chihuahua mix who lived for 15 years with Elin D. Stockman, an office assistant in Wisconsin, whose hobbies are gardening, decorating, and painting.

Many years ago, a friend surprised me by giving me a tiny, black, adorable puppy named Spooky. She weighed only seven pounds, and being such a little dog, I could easily put her into my purse or shirt pocket. Everywhere I went, she went. We were so close it felt as if we shared one soul. One of my favorite places to take her was Butterfly Beach, a beautiful, spacious area where she could frolic and try to catch butterflies. She loved to run and chase anything or anyone, barking all the while in her coloratura soprano voice.

Despite her small size, Spooky was not easily intimidated. When my dad would lie down on the floor to growl and bark at her, she would respond in kind and never take her eyes off him. Spooky also had this "I'll do what I want, when I want" attitude. After I was married, my husband brought his two larger dogs into our family. One day they were sitting, waiting patiently for permission to devour their treats, which had been placed on the floor in front of them. Spooky suddenly appeared out of nowhere, grabbed both treats, and was out of sight again before I knew it! The two well-behaved dogs sat there in disbelief. How could that have happened? While they were being polite, that brat Spooky had stolen their goodies!

My little vixen remained healthy and active until her last year of life, when she developed congestive heart failure. She had always been so full of energy that I had deluded myself into thinking she would go on forever. When her kidneys began to fail and she became very ill, I felt fearful and panicky, wondering how I could live without her. In a desperate attempt to keep her alive, I put her on kidney dialysis. By the second treatment, however, it became apparent that she would not get better. Finally resigned to her fate, I brought her home, thinking this would be the best place for her to die. After three days, I changed my mind, and knew she should be euthanized as soon as possible. Unfortunately, my vets were out of town, and the only available place to go was the emergency hospital. Completely torn about what to do, I prayed for an answer or a sign. As I finished my prayer, a nearby light bulb fizzled and went out. Immediately thereafter, the phone rang! A good friend was calling me because he sensed that something was wrong. We discussed my dilemma and both felt that I should take Spooky to the emergency hospital. I told my husband about my decision, and out of love and concern, he went with me.

When the vet came in to euthanize Spooky, a white cloud of protection seemed to envelop us, taking away my ability to focus on all that was happening. I seemed to hear the vet's voice, but not her words. Spooky was euthanized, and my husband and I stayed with her. The protective bubble seemed to be around us for about an hour, but when it disappeared, I knew that Spooky's soul had departed from her body. My husband and I left, grief-stricken.

Early the next day, I went to retrieve Spooky's dead body from the vet. As ghoulish as it may sound, I had to have her with me, no matter what the circumstances. Bringing her into the house turned out to be a blessing for my family. Even my mother, who was initially appalled at the idea of a dead body in the house, remarked how beautiful Spooky looked, wrapped in her blanket. Later that day, I took Spooky to be cremated, and that very evening, I picked up her ashes. I just couldn't bear to be without her!

As the days passed, it was all I could do to go on. I was angry with God for letting me have such a wonderful little companion and then taking her away. I even wondered if I had done something to deserve losing her. Then, about ten months after Spooky's death, I had an incredibly realistic dream. I still remember every detail and image even though it happened over a year ago. In the dream, I found myself in an unfamiliar house, along with the two dogs that had lived with Spooky and me after I was married. I suddenly felt apprehensive and wondered where Spooky was. Immediately, she came flying into the room, looking so healthy, so black, and so young. As I lay down on my stomach to be close to my tiny girl, she came and kissed me on the nose, her trademark behavior. I felt her wet tongue, and as I looked into her face, I noticed that her cataracts were gone. Then I woke up. The dream was short but powerful. I felt as though I had truly been with her. After seeing and feeling Spooky again, I knew without a doubt that she would always be with me.

A second contact was even more amazing. It occurred just before the first anniversary of Spooky's death. I awoke early one morning, which was unusual for me. From my bed, I could see the portion of our living room that led to the front door. Apparently my husband had fallen asleep, leaving the television on. There, sitting on the living room floor in the light from the TV screen, was Spooky! Unsure of what I was seeing, I rubbed my eyes and put my glasses on. Sure enough, she was there! She appeared to be solid, but her image quivered like an old-time movie, probably due to the flickering light from the television. I watched her from my bed for a moment, and for the entire time, she remained motionless, looking toward the front door. I kept thinking, "I don't believe this! Is this real? Could this actually be happening?" Surprisingly, I took the entire experience very much in stride and went back to sleep as soon as she disappeared.

Later, I questioned why I had reacted so calmly when I saw her. Why didn't I try to get her attention, or get out of bed and go to her? Then I realized that I had finally come to accept that Spooky was where she was supposed to be, in another dimension.

To keep her memory close to me, I wear three tattoos of Spooky. The first is a drawing of her face, along with her name. The second is a side view, showing her with a halo and wings, and the third, written on my leg, is "I miss you, Spooky." Shortly after Spooky died, I wrote to the friend who had given her to me, thanking him again for this special gift.

Petunia and *Taffy*

...Toy Poodles who belonged to Margaret DeLuca of New Jersey, and entertained her while she enjoyed her favorite hobbies, knitting and reading. Petunia lived to be almost 14, and Taffy lived to be 15.

Our first Toy Poodle, Petunia, was an affectionate little imp who weighed about nine pounds. She had a beautiful silvery gray coat, and for 12 years I took her to Lenore's shop for grooming. Petunia always managed to entertain everyone in the grooming shop with her mischievous pranks. As soon as she got into her cage, the little rascal would deliberately pull her leash through one of the openings. Next, she would extend her paw out of the cage and knock over any bottles and cans that were sitting on the counter. Whenever she succeeded in tipping things over or knocking them off the shelf, she would glance around quickly to see if anyone was paying attention to her! It was obvious that Petunia loved being a clown and the center of attention. Even as she became older, her sense of humor and desire to be in the limelight never left her.

After Petunia died, our house seemed so empty that my husband and I decided not to wait too long before we got another Toy Poodle. We named our new puppy Taffy. She was beige and grew up to be small, like Petunia, weighing only about eight pounds. Although Taffy looked a lot like Petunia, she acted more bossy and spoiled. She was a yappy little dog, always letting us know what she wanted and when she wanted it! As soon as her water bowl was empty, she would hit it with her paw. Whenever we left her alone, she would get angry and throw pillows on the floor. Apparently she thought she owned our bed, because she would become annoyed if either my husband or I dared to crowd into "her space." The little brat would push us with her feet, demanding that we move over to give her more room!

Taffy was taken to the same grooming shop as Petunia. It wasn't long before Lenore noticed some startling similarities between the two Poodles. Lenore told me, "When I first saw Taffy, I was surprised at how much she looked like Petunia, except for her color, of course. The two dogs had the same expression and were the same size, with similar body shape, muzzle, and eyes. But their similarities in appearance paled in comparison to the identical way they behaved in my grooming shop! When Taffy first came into my place, I was astonished to see her pull her leash into her cage,

just as Petunia had done. And like Petunia, she reached out with her paw and pushed over any containers that sat next to the cage. Afterward she surveyed the area to see if anyone was watching her. Taffy always repeated these actions *exactly* like her predecessor! It is mind-boggling that two unrelated dogs would perform these unusual behaviors in precisely the same way. Throughout my thirty-one years of grooming, I've never seen another dog behave like these two Poodles!" Lenore told me on more than one occasion, "Mrs. DeLuca, you have not lost Petunia because she has been reincarnated into Taffy! Or else Petunia is telling Taffy what to do! "

Now Taffy is gone and my house feels empty again. Lenore really misses both dogs, too, and no longer gets nearly as much exercise as she used to, from bending and picking up cans and bottles knocked off the shelf. By the way, neither Petunia nor Taffy was trained to push over containers, and Taffy never met Petunia to learn these tricks from her. Was this just a coincidence? Is there really such a thing as reincarnation, or can the dead send messages to the living? Perhaps someday I will know the answers.

"It is the secret of the world that all things subsist and do not die, but only retire a little from sight and afterwards return again."

…Ralph Waldo Emerson

Wolf

...a Collie-Malamute mix, rescued from the Rhode Island pound by Stacey Greenberg, a biology teacher and dog trainer. Wolf lived to be 14 years old.

It was the middle of the afternoon on July 4th, and almost everyone was out for the day, probably boating or fishing or picnicking. I was reading in the living room of my apartment, and my dog, Wolf, was snoozing at my feet, dreaming of cookies and love pats. The peaceful afternoon was suddenly interrupted when someone turned my doorknob several times. I was glad that I always kept my door locked, despite the quiet neighborhood. When I heard the heavy footsteps of someone leaving the building, I ran to the window to see if I could identify the person who had neither rung the bell nor knocked on the door. There was a tall, dark man I had never seen before, walking to the side of the building. Thinking he might just have gone to the

wrong apartment, I put a leash on Wolf and stepped out onto my front porch, intending to give the stranger directions. The man was returning to my apartment, looking down at the ground when I asked him, "Who are you looking for?"

"I'm looking for a place to rent," he replied as he glanced quickly at me. I don't think he saw the dog at first, but suddenly his eyes locked onto Wolf. My dog was usually tolerant of people, but this time he became agitated and began to bark and lunge at the man repeatedly. The man turned and walked away quickly, and Wolf and I were both relieved.

That evening, Wolf and I sat close together and enjoyed the July 4th fireworks display. He was the only dog I have ever known who *loved* to watch fireworks. He sat next to me, enthralled by the lights, and I wondered if he could see the colors. The noises never seemed to bother him as they did other dogs. Warm July evenings always remind me of sitting close together with Wolf, watching the fireworks like two human beings. A few days later, I heard that the police had picked up a man of our stranger's description because of "suspicious activity" in our neighborhood.

Wolf and I had been together for only about four months when he protected me from that man. We met while I was studying biology in graduate school and working as a volunteer at the local animal shelter. I would come in on Saturday and take the dogs out for a walk. As I was living in a small apartment and busy with classes, I was not expecting to get a dog of my own. Then I spotted Wolf. He was the most regal dog I had ever seen, and just looking at him took my breath away. I couldn't wait to take him for our first walk, and I brought a ball along in case he knew how to fetch. He was still a baby according to his paperwork, just over a year old, and his previous owner's reason for giving him up was vague. I threw the ball and both of us began to run toward it. I'll never forget that as we were running together, Wolf looked at me with a surprised and delighted expression. I could imagine that he was thinking, "Hey! We're doing this together!" It made me think that no one had ever played with him before. He seemed to have experienced a revelation, because after that magical moment, his eye contact with me was intense. Before, he had been looking through me with little interest, but now he really saw me. After our time together, I reluctantly took him back to his cage. He started howling pathetically as soon as I turned to leave. There was no question that we had made a definite connection. I *had* to adopt him! He was the special dog I had always hoped for, and I wasn't going to let him slip away.

Before I could bring Wolf home, I needed to find another apartment, one that would allow dogs. In the interim, I boarded him and visited as often as possible. I think he wondered why I couldn't take him with me. Whenever I came to see him, Wolf would come running and stand up on his hind legs, putting his paws on my shoulders so he could look directly into my eyes, as if he were asking that question.

Once Wolf was home with me, we did everything together. We went to the park and played retrieve and tug o' war, and I took him for many long walks. Once off leash, he loved to run ahead, but he came back frequently to make sure I was still around. Sometimes I would hide from him and watch as he became terribly concerned about where I was. Then I would stand up and he would come flying in my direction. Occasionally, I would turn and run away from him, and that excited him even more. When he got to me, we jumped around together, and I laughed with delight, so happy to have such a friend.

Despite our strong connection, Wolf retained an air of independence. He liked being petted and tolerated being hugged, but he was not "Mr. Cuddly," always wanting to sit on my lap. Just as well, since he weighed more than 90 pounds! He was protective of me, especially on our walks, always standing between any stranger and me. His size and demeanor discouraged anyone who might want to hurt us.

Nine months after I acquired Wolf, I bought "Panda," a three-month-old Lab-Whippet mix. Now that I had two dogs, I moved into a house, which had a large backyard and a fence that extended all around one side of the house as well as across the back. Wolf and Panda loved to run and chase each other. Hoping that Wolf would pursue her, Panda would zoom like a maniac across the backyard and around to the side yard and then return to the back, repeating her game over and over again. Wolf would chase her awhile, but her streamlined figure always left him trailing. Then Wolf introduced the element of surprise into the game. He would stop just out of Panda's sight and jump out at her as she came tearing around the corner. Afterward they would roll and wrestle, and if they had been two kids, they would have been laughing the entire time.

The dogs were similar in many ways, but Panda was high-strung, while Wolf radiated serenity and peace, a "Zen essence." Just looking at him made me feel calm, no matter what was irritating me. He was always there to soothe my anxieties while I was a student, and afterward, too, when I was working on my own. During my brief two-year marriage and subsequent divorce, Wolf became my anchor as I endured the sadness and aggravation related to these changes in my life. In truth, Wolf had always been my anchor, but it became especially apparent at this time.

When Wolf was about 12, I brought home a Belgian Sheepdog named Kestry, who proved to be a livelier companion for Panda. Less than two years later, Wolf developed arthritis, and even getting up and walking was painful for him. He also suffered a grand mal seizure followed by many petit mal episodes, and over time they took their toll on him mentally and physically. His appetite was still good and, to some extent, he still enjoyed life, but we no longer went for walks, and he had lost interest in playing ball. His health was deteriorating steadily, and I wanted more than anything else for Wolf to die with dignity. After agonizing deliberation, I decided to have him euthanized. The vet was kind enough to come to my house, and as we all gathered in the kitchen, he gave Wolf the injection. Afterward, he left me alone to say goodbye to my friend.

Losing my longtime buddy was devastating emotionally, but I was completely unprepared for what happened next. As I knelt by Wolf's body, a feeling of intense joy swept over me. The overwhelming grief was replaced by sheer exuberance, and the feeling was not coming from within me, but rather from outside – from Wolf! *He was the joy!* He was celebrating his being set free and released from his pain. It could not have been clearer. I threw my head back and almost laughed aloud. I had done the right thing! I had ended the suffering of my dearest friend.

I could have been content forever, just remembering that special moment, but others were yet to come when I least expected them. I needed a family of three canines again, so I adopted Phoenix, a young Australian Shepherd. I had not forgotten about Wolf, and I was certainly not trying to replace him, but having three dogs just felt right. Late one afternoon about a year after Wolf's death, I was standing behind my couch watching something on the news, when I suddenly sensed the presence of a dog next to me. I automatically reached down to pet him as I continued to look at the television. My hand felt the warmth and fur of the dog, and I petted him for a few seconds before it hit me that all three of my dogs were outside. I was momentarily startled, because the dog I had been petting had a distinct bump at the top of its skull, just as Wolf's had. I remember thinking, "It must be Wolf!" I dared not look down, knowing it might interrupt the experience I was enjoying. The images on the television faded away as I focused my attention completely on my hand, which continued to feel Wolf's head for another ten seconds or more. Then the sensation disappeared. I looked down, but saw nothing. Then I ran to check on my other three dogs. Just as I remembered, they were all outside!

Not long after that, another interesting thing happened. One evening I went by myself to see a friend who was also involved in dog training. It was just beginning to get dark as I drove into the parking lot where we had planned to meet. "Hi, Stacey," she called. "Which dog did you bring?" I told her I hadn't brought any, but she swore she had seen a large dog sitting in the backseat. Wolf always sat in the backseat of my car and watched over my shoulder as I drove!

I had held his dead body in my arms and felt the deepest joy of my life. I had touched his head and knew that we were still connected. I had heard my friend's certainty that she had seen him in the car. Now I am convinced that Wolf still exists in some form. Death is not oblivion or loss of self. Something continues, and we all exist in eternity after we die.

Rudy

...an incredibly beautiful and intelligent Miniature Poodle who lived for all but four months of his 14 years with Dr. Ann Redding. She is a retired professor of biology, whose hobbies are dog training and gardening, and whose passion is agility!

What a profound effect this dog had on my life! He taught me about love and respect, he changed the way I train my dogs, and ultimately, he inspired me to write this book.

This unforgettable little dog came into my life when he was four months old. Luckily for me, a breeder in Fresno was willing to sell him because one of his testicles had not descended. She had hoped to show him in conformation, but that was not to be. When I first saw him, I was disappointed in his appearance. He had a lot of straight, coarse black hair and a really long muzzle, and he appeared to have short legs. He looked like a mop with a nose! All that didn't seem to matter because I bought him that day and named him Rudy.

By the time he was nine months old, my "ugly duckling" had grown to be a regal, well-proportioned Miniature Poodle. He was a proud little guy with a distinctly "macho" presence and attitude, and he walked with a swagger that let everyone know that "he be da man!" Being domineering and somewhat aggressive, he enjoyed placing a toy or treat strategically between his front paws and then growling whenever my other dogs passed by. If Rudy was in the car and the windshield wipers were moving, he always barked ferociously and tried to bite them. He also came unglued if anyone attempted to wash the car windows or peered into a window that was closed! My friend Tom and I loved to tease him whenever he sat in the car, because his reaction was so predictable! One day I put on a hand puppet and pretended it was barking at him. As expected, Rudy bristled, lunged, and bit the puppet!

At the age of nine, Rudy experienced his most outstanding and memorable "machismo moment." An unfamiliar, loose Pit Bull approached me boldly as I was walking my four Poodles in the neighborhood. All my dogs started barking and pulling on their leashes while I screamed as loudly as I could, absolutely certain that the Pit Bull was going to attack. Rudy pulled so hard that his collar came loose. He lunged at the intruder. Feelings of fear and helplessness surged through me as I called for help, certain that Rudy was going to be killed. Instead, the Pit Bull turned away and ran back down the street, with Rudy chasing him and nipping at his heels! By then, my neighbors had come out to see what all the commotion was. Applause and cheers filled the air as Rudy returned for his "victory lap." I was just glad he was safe and that I could take him home.

In truth, my ferocious little Rudy was bluffing. Underneath all that bravado, he was something of a chicken. If you accidentally stepped on his toe, he screamed bloody murder and walked on three legs, holding the offended paw as if it had been damaged for life. One day he got into a scuffle with a female dog in the neighborhood, and when she got the better of him, he came back running and crying, even though there wasn't a scratch on him.

I had hoped to train Rudy to be a great obedience dog, but he didn't seem to enjoy the exercises. Looking back, I believe his attitude was my fault. Not knowing any better, I used negative reinforcement, which was the accepted method of training at that time. The struggle between us really began when I got to the "ear pinch." Rudy fought back by whining, barking, and even biting me on several occasions. In some perverse way, I think the little guy sensed my frustration and enjoyed the struggle. Knowing what I know now, I would never have used these techniques on a dog, especially one like Rudy.

Eventually my proud boy earned his obedience trial championship (OTCH). Ironically, his last trial occurred on his tenth birthday. It was probably a birthday present he gave to himself! I can imagine him thinking, "Whew . . . now I don't have to do these exercises anymore." I felt the same way. By that time, I deeply regretted having used such a negative method to train him.

After the OTCH, I continued to train Rudy, but my style had changed. I never forced him to do anything. I began to "listen" to him, and as we interacted, I became more aware of what he was "telling" me. To get Rudy to do the exercises willingly and enthusiastically, I had to become a motivational trainer, because no master-slave arrangement would work well with this dog.

Rudy taught me that any training that can't be accomplished primarily with a calm attitude, affection, play, or food is not worth doing! Gradually, the struggle between us gave way to a sweet and non-combative relationship. Rudy became an attentive, loving companion, who played retrieve and tug with me, did some agility, and even did obedience happily. If I packed my suitcases, he was the first of my dogs to jump into the car. When I left the house to do errands, he always ran outside to the gate to watch me leave, and there he

waited by himself, sometimes for hours, until I returned. We were partners. Finally, I began to understand what love is. It took a special dog to teach me.

When Rudy was 11, he developed laryngeal paralysis, a condition that made it difficult for him to breathe. To correct the problem, I opted for a surgery to create a permanent opening into his trachea and lungs. That procedure, unfortunately, made him vulnerable to aspiration pneumonia. After Rudy endured a severe bout of pneumonia, I diligently fed him by hand and put his water on an elevated surface to ensure that whatever he ingested went into his stomach and not into his lungs. He had great quality of life despite his health problem, and I was determined to keep him alive, healthy, and happy as long as possible. Knowing that our time together was precious, I spent many hours taking Rudy for long walks, practicing agility, and playing tug of war or "retrieve the tennis ball " with him.

One day we were sitting on the bed together when he began to kiss my face. Kissing was something Rudy did often, but this time it was different. The licking went on and on, and he was so insistent that it was difficult to stop him! Even when I pushed him away, he kept coming back, and I remember thinking how strangely he was behaving. Now I wonder if he knew he was going to die, and this was his way of saying, "I love you," and "Goodbye."

A few days later, I found Rudy lying motionless on his side. As he had not eaten breakfast, I thought he might have fainted from low blood sugar. Once I fed him, he seemed to recover and to gain strength. I left to buy some enzymes for him, thinking he might be having digestive problems. When I returned home, I was relieved to see the little guy waiting for me by the gate. As soon as he saw the car, he rushed into the house to greet me. As usual, I played tug with him and then gave him the toy, which he promptly and proudly carried through the house for all the other dogs to see. Then it was time for us to go outside. When I opened the kitchen door, all the dogs ran out except Rudy. He stood in the threshold looking out at the backyard. The breeze was gently blowing his ears. Suddenly he had a seizure.

I was frantic. Immediately, I took him to the veterinary hospital where he had been treated before. While we waited to see the vet, he sat on my lap, washing my face with continuous kisses. The vet seemed optimistic, believing that Rudy could be helped. Relieved, I left him at the hospital for observation and to have some tests done. Two hours later, the phone rang. It was the vet, calling with the shocking news that Rudy had suffered a severe seizure and was unconscious.

When I saw Rudy the next day, he was in a coma. He wasn't responding well to any of the medications and was still having seizures. The vet thought he probably had a brain lesion, and she warned me that Rudy's prognosis was poor.

His illness was so sudden and so unbearable for me. I had hoped to have him for at least two more years. As I sobbed and hugged him, I thought about my options. I was alarmed because he was still having seizures, and I was worried that he might be suffering. For that reason, and because of his age, I decided not to put him through any more tests or procedures. I knew euthanasia was best for him, and I held him as he slipped away; afterward, I cried uncontrollably. I took his body to the pet cemetery for cremation, but when I got there, I couldn't bear to part with him. To ease my pain, I cut off large chunks of his hair and stuffed them into a plastic bag to keep a part of him with me.

Rudy's sudden death caused me to plummet into a state of profound grief. Overwhelmed by feelings of despair and periods of crying, I reached out to friends and family to help me get through this difficult period.

Sometimes I felt the sadness was going to explode inside me and that I wasn't going to survive. Even with pills, I could sleep only three or four hours.

Three days after Rudy's death, I woke up at just past midnight. Knowing I could not go back to sleep, I went to the quiet room where I meditate. There I cried and prayed in the silent darkness for almost an hour. Afterward I felt peaceful and numb, and continued to sit quietly on the floor. Then I heard soft but distinct sounds, as if fingernails were gently scratching or brushing against the wall. Three times in a row, the scratching was repeated. Seconds later, the same soft scratching came again, three times in a row, just as before. It was familiar...the same gentle way that Rudy used to scratch on the door. "Oh, my God," I thought, "it's Rudy!" I got up quickly, calling his name as I headed toward the sound. It appeared to be coming from the hall or laundry room, both of which were close to the room in which I had been meditating. I moved closer to the sound, which was repeated again in the same pattern. When I got to the laundry room, I stood still, but there was only silence.

Standing in my dark, quiet house, I thought about what I had heard. It didn't sound like a rat or a mouse. The sounds were too subtle and rhythmic. The scratching couldn't have come from my other dogs, who were asleep on the other side of the house. Perhaps it was the wind brushing something against the house, or maybe it was raining. I stepped outside into a clear, still night, and finally accepted the reality of my encounter with Rudy. Joy and gratitude swept over me as I concluded that Rudy must still exist in some form and be conscious and aware or he could not have communicated with me! This event turned out to be one of the most significant in my life.

The next morning, my five-month-old pup, Tiffany, suddenly began to bark wildly. She was looking into the hallway, focused exactly on the area where I had heard the scratching! Although nothing unusual was visible, she appeared to be alarmed, and her barking was loud and continuous. After a while, she stopped barking and moved cautiously toward the area to investigate. Apparently finding nothing, she ran to me, begging for her breakfast. A few hours later, I was in the backyard with my dogs, where, a week before, I had lightly trimmed their hair, and Rudy's. As I looked down, I was surprised to see a clump of black and gray hair clinging to the front of my Levis. I knew it was Rudy's, but it could not have been the hair I had saved in a plastic bag; it could not have belonged to my other Poodles, as they are solidly white, brown, or black without a trace of gray. I am always careful to pick up any hair I trim and no hair was visible in the grass. I tossed the hair aside, but it came right back and stuck to my jeans. Again I picked it up and discarded it, but again it returned. "Okay, Rudy, I'm keeping it," I said. Now this special clump of hair rests with Rudy's cremated ashes in my meditation room, symbolizing the message that Rudy is "sticking" with me.

As time went by, I continued to experience those sad moments, and I often wondered if Rudy's spirit was still visiting me. Finally, I asked him to give me a specific sign, one that would be real evidence of his presence. The image of a black ball popped into my head. I forgot about my request until one morning a few days later as I was washing my face, I noticed something black on the bathroom counter, something that didn't belong there. "What is this black ball doing here?" I mumbled aloud. Then, realizing what I had just said, I was stunned. I had no idea how this small ball of dog hair or yarn got onto my bathroom counter. This wasn't the "black ball" I had envisioned as a sign, but my spontaneous verbalization made me believe that it was, indeed, the contact I had asked Rudy to give me.

I have no doubt that Rudy's afterlife contacts were acts of love, designed to ease my grief. He came to reassure me that he still existed and was around me. His visitations amazed and exhilarated me, even though the pain of loss still lingered. Other less dramatic contacts with Rudy occurred and piqued my interest in the afterlife. I began to read about the subject, and eventually decided to contact a spiritual medium. A spiritual medium is one who claims to be able to receive messages from deceased souls, and to pass them on to loved ones during a séance.

I made an appointment with a reputable medium, Brian Hurst, who is probably best known for discovering and teaching the well-known medium, James van Praagh. Van Praagh has written several books concerning communication with the dead, and he has also been the moving force behind the television show "Ghost Whisperer." I met Brian in his home one evening, hoping I might hear something from my deceased father and my pets, especially Rudy. There were ten people in our group for the three-hour session. I was the last to have a reading. Brian spoke about my deceased father and the close bond we shared. The word "architecture" came up several times, and the name "Jerry" or "Gary." It meant nothing to me, and I left the séance thinking that Brian had very little correct information about me. I felt quite skeptical about the validity of the reading, but as I walked to the car, I suddenly recalled that the day before, I had met with the architectural committee to inspect a house owned by a man named Gary! I had been the head of the Homeowner's Association for more than a year. How could I have forgotten that? How could Brian have known it? Was my father aware of my activities, and was he passing ideas to the medium? I thought about the séance all the way home.

Once home, I opened the back door to put the four Poodles outside. Then a bizarre and spooky thing happened — a bat flew into my house! The creature flew around for 20 minutes before it found the open door and disappeared into the night. "First the séance and then a bat," I thought. I had recovered the significance of "architecture" and "Jerry," and I had been visited by a creature who is often associated with "the dark arts." The events of the evening left no doubt in my mind that I would be visiting the medium again soon.

A second visit to Brian yielded additional correct information about my father, my house, and my life. Interestingly, he mentioned that I was writing a book. My heart skipped a beat when Brian asked, "Is there a Ruby or Ruthie?"

"You are very close to the name," I said, hoping he would continue, but he could not.

"It's faint and I'm not getting anything more. I'll have to move on," Brian declared apologetically.

I went back a third time, hoping to hear more about Rudy. My deceased father appeared again, and this time Brian gave a perfect description of my mother. Again he asked, "Is there a Ruby...or Ruthie...or Rudy?"

"Yes! There is a Rudy!" I replied. By now my heart was pounding in anticipation.

Oh, yes. Rudy. That is what I'm hearing." Brian started to say something else, but he hesitated and was quiet.

Seconds went by as I waited anxiously. Finally I couldn't stand the suspense and blurted out, "He's not human!"

The room was silent. Brian stood quietly and looked toward the ceiling. He appeared to be concentrating intently, trying to receive a message. A minute or two passed, and nothing was said. Then Brian's expression began to change; he smiled and nodded his head slightly, as if to indicate that he understood. He turned to me and exclaimed confidently, "Ah...Rudy. Rudy is a little dog, and your father has him."

There was a gasp from the group as they shared my joy. Relief and gratitude spread through me. Tears welled up and I wept. What a moment that was for me! Such sweet words I had heard. Now I knew that Rudy was with my father on the "Other Side."

As time went by, I came to appreciate how much Rudy had taught me. What irony! I had always thought I was the teacher, instructing him in obedience and working hard to make him do what I wanted. Now I know he was the teacher, helping me to change and become more compassionate and loving. I write about Rudy to honor him and to reveal the amazing mystical things that happened after he died. I have frequently shed tears of humility and gratitude for the changes that have occurred in me as a result of knowing this unforgettable dog.

Bruno

...an easygoing black Lab-mix dog, sweet and affectionate, without a mean bone in his body. He lived in Wisconsin for ten years with his friend Robin Bone, a retail manager and collector of toys.

One day, my friend Michael surprised me with the gift of a beautiful eight-week-old puppy. The pup had been abandoned in a shopping mall parking lot about three weeks earlier, and he had been sheltered and bottle-fed by personnel at the Humane Society until he was old enough to go to a new home. My new canine friend was a black Lab mix, and we could tell by the size of his feet that he was going to be a *big* guy, so we named him Bruno.

About a year later, we added a yellow Lab mix puppy to our family, a female that we called Murphy. We hoped that Murphy would be the perfect companion for Bruno, and indeed she was. The two dogs became best friends, running constantly, chasing one another, playing tug of war, and finally collapsing in a weary heap to take a nap together. It was touching to watch them share everything, right down to their rawhide bones. I always made a point of buying two large rawhides so that each dog would have one. The dogs, however, had their own idea about how the treats should be eaten.

Bruno would chew on one bone first, while Murphy watched. As soon as the rawhide became soft and gooey, Murphy would move in close to Bruno. Then Bruno would drop the rawhide, as if to say, "Okay, Murphy. Here it is. I've got it nice and soft for you. You can take it now." Murphy would pick up the gooey bone, bite big chunks from it, and swallow them. Meanwhile, Bruno would get the other rawhide and chew that one for a bit before letting Murphy finish it off. That was their routine, every time. There were never any arguments or fighting, as each dog had a role to play in the rawhide demolition.

I am the manager of a furniture store, and my office is a large, comfortable room at the back. By the time Bruno was five and Murphy was four, the two of them came to work with me every day. They snoozed together while I worked and entertained me when I took a break. They were never any trouble, and were clearly content being with me, just "hanging out."

After work, I would take them for a walk. Bruno was a quiet, mellow dog who never left my side, so he never needed a leash. Murphy, on the other hand, was rambunctious and tended to wander, so she needed a sturdy, leather one. Since Bruno loved to have something in his mouth, it was easy to train him to hold onto Murphy's leash. That's how we took our evening walks. I would stroll along with Bruno beside me, while Bruno held Murphy in check! Everyone who saw the dogs was amused by their actions and found it quite entertaining to watch our little "parade."

For a special outing, I would take them across the street to a big schoolyard, where they could run and play ball with me. I would throw the tennis ball and they would retrieve it until it was a soggy, slimy mess! In the winter, Michael and I would go sledding with the dogs. Bruno would sit in the sled as we sailed about halfway down the hill, but then he would jump out and sometimes tumble until he could stand and slide down on all four feet. It was great fun. The dogs were like children to us.

One particular winter day, when Michael and I took the dogs for a walk, Bruno was doing what he loved most – chasing ducks across a frozen pond. He was about eight years old then, and probably weighed 115 pounds. Suddenly the ice gave way, and he fell through it. He tried to climb out, but the icy surface was too slippery. We panicked, wondering how to get Bruno out of this predicament. We had no idea how deep the water was, but we knew it was very cold. Clearly, there was only one way to extricate Bruno – one of us would have to pull him out! Michael grabbed the dog's rear end and began to tug, while I cheered him on. Bruno seemed unconcerned and not panicky in the least, trusting that we would rescue him. With tremendous effort, Michael pulled and pulled until finally he yanked Bruno out of the hole in the ice. By the time they both emerged, they were soaking wet and freezing. After the dog was out of danger and we were all home again, Michael and I sat in front of a blazing fire, drinking hot chocolate and reminiscing about what had happened. The exhausted Labs were snoozing. We began to laugh about how ridiculous Michael had looked, trying to keep his footing on the frozen pond while pulling on this big, wet black dog who didn't seem to have a care in the world!

When Bruno was about ten, he came to the furniture store with me one Sunday afternoon. We hadn't been there long when he suddenly urinated on the floor, something he had never done before. Suspecting that he had a bladder infection, I took him to the veterinary clinic the following day. The staff urged me to leave Bruno with them for testing. When I answered the phone on Tuesday, they gave me the horrible news that Bruno had a malignant tumor pressing against his urethra and he could no longer control the flow of his urine. One option was to remove the tumor and attach a bag to collect the urine. I was certainly willing to try it, knowing that many human beings undergo similar procedures, but the vet cautioned me that the cancer was aggressive, and he didn't think that Bruno would live more than a few weeks. What a shock that was! I called Michael for advice and support, and together we agreed, reluctantly, that Bruno should be euthanized.

We called to tell the vet of our decision, and then took Bruno out to be with us for the last time. We made the occasion special by bringing along his pal Murphy. It all seemed surreal. Bruno acted healthy, energetic, and so pleased to be with us, as if there was nothing wrong. We took a little walk and played ball for a while and then Michael took Bruno inside the clinic and stayed with him while he was put down. I wanted to be with Bruno, too, but his sudden illness and my lack of experience with death overwhelmed me. I didn't feel that I could handle being there. Later on, I came to regret that decision deeply. Not only did I have to cope with the grief of losing this wonderful dog, I had to face my guilt for not being there for him. I felt extremely depressed.

About two months after Bruno's passing, I woke up in the middle of the night for no apparent reason. There, as usual, was Bruno, lying on the pillows close to my face! I could see him clearly because the aquarium light in my bedroom stays on all night. I reached out and touched Bruno's head, and in return, he kissed my face. "Wait a minute!" I thought, as a strange feeling came over me. I sat up abruptly in bed, realizing this couldn't be happening. Bruno was dead! For a moment, I wondered if I had mistaken Murphy for Bruno, but then I saw her asleep as always at the foot of my bed. I looked back quickly at the pillow where I had seen Bruno, but he was gone.

How could I have seen Bruno? I lay back and recalled how guilty I felt about the hasty way we had euthanized him, and how I had regretted not being with him during his transition. Those sentiments seem to fade away with Bruno's visit, and now I was left with comfort and amazement. Bruno had come and I had touched him and he had kissed my face. I was reassured that he was all right with the manner of his death, and that he understood why I was unable to be with him. After that, I could focus on the many happy times we had together. Thank you, Bruno, for being such a wonderful companion in life, and for returning after death to teach me an important lesson: we do not lose the ones we love; they are always with us.

Robbie and *Feeny*

...two irrepressible Shelties who stole the heart and filled the life of Ann Campbell, a high school English and journalism teacher, in Denver. Robbie lived until his tenth birthday, and Feeny lived 12 years. After them came the Argyll Shelties, a kennel well-known for its many sound and beautiful champions.

Memories of my inadequacy as a dog owner when I first met that little black Shetland Sheepdog still make me laugh. He was the last of a litter of seven born in the wee hours of the morning of May 28, 1967. There were six pups when my friend Jo cleaned her sable Sheltie, Aqui, and put everyone to bed, but in the morning, there he was! I met him when he was just a week old. He was the one who snuggled into my hand as if to let me know he wanted me. I wasn't at all sure I wanted him – I'd never owned a dog! My friends said I needed him, and I had birthday money from my brother, Robert, so I bought the pup and named him Robbie. When he was six weeks old, Jo had to leave for a summer program in her field of teaching, so all the pups went to their new homes. I put Robbie on the front seat of the car, and told him that he was always to sit there, on the passenger side. Apparently he understood, because he sat quietly in that spot all the way home. Later that day, he tolerated my ineptness as I walked him to the park on the end of a *very heavy* chain-link lead, which was attached to an infinitesimally small red harness. A man who passed us joked, "Don't let that tiger get away from you!"

Robbie learned very quickly! He learned that we were not just going out to stroll aimlessly up and down the street in the middle of the night, accompanied by the security guard of the apartment, so he was housebroken by eight weeks! He learned that when the doorbell rang and I opened our apartment door, he could *fly* down the hallway and leap into the arms of one of my friends and do his funny growl and grumble that made him sound so fierce! He learned that the lonely hours of his day could be spent sleeping, playing with toys, or chewing on rawhide, but that books and magazines, which made such lovely confetti, were not his property. He learned not to sit on the sprinkler head outside our dining room window, where I could tie him and see him while I cleaned the house. One day the sprinkler came on, and he was shot into the air on a jet of water! He learned to stay out of the pine pitch at the cabin where we spent the summer, because it was no fun at all having his feet cleaned!

Robbie's favorite time of day was whenever I was at home, and especially when I came home after school and took him to the park on my bicycle. He rode in a large wicker basket trimmed with flowers, and we played ball from the time we arrived until we were both exhausted and ready to ride home, with a stop for ice cream at the Purity Dairy. Once he ran a splinter up under his ribs. There was no visible wound, but an abscess formed a terrifying lump, which even his doctor thought might be cancer. Robbie was such a favorite at the hospital that they had a party when surgery revealed that it wasn't! He was such a chicken about getting shots! The doctor always laughed when he had just touched him with the cotton, and Robbie began screaming and tried to climb on my shoulder. He always had a rather delicate stomach, but his only serious surgery was a tonsillectomy when he was just a year old.

I thought Robbie was the cutest puppy I had ever seen, with his dear little face, black ears, reddish-brown eyebrows, a white blaze from mouth to forehead, and a white tuxedo front. He was like a little stuffed toy, and I simply couldn't get enough of looking at him. Later, it was pointed out to me that my beloved Sheltie had numerous "faults" and would never be a show dog. He was an inch too tall, but fine boned. He had a very wavy coat. His under jaw was too narrow, and his upper jaw a bit too long, so that he had buck teeth! Undoubtedly, his best physical feature was his perfectly tipped ears. None of that mattered to me. He was mine, and I loved him. I thought he was gorgeous, and I was proud to take him to obedience classes offered by the local Sheltie club. He was a total goof-off, even though we "practiced" at home for hours every evening! Even the instructor cracked up at Robbie's antics.

If he never got to be a show dog, he made up for it by starring on the stage at South High in rallies, assemblies, and in the All-School Show, *Carnival*. He played the role of "Rover," the dog who danced with "Pav-lover," and wore a nylon net tutu, a cone-shaped hat trimmed with net, and a striped T-shirt. He pretended to be mortified by the costume until he heard the applause the first night. Then he ran to the footlights and did a Sheltie "bow," and the audience went wild! Although he couldn't have explained a "standing ovation," he got one after every performance as he repeated his bow!

He was always a ham! Whenever I packed a suitcase, he became pitifully lame, and when I left him for *any* reason, even for going to work, he would lie on his back with all four paws stiff in the air, mourning before I ever closed the door. When he was seven months old, I left him with his breeder while I went home for Christmas. For the first three days, Robbie stayed pressed against the inside of the back door of her house, where I had said goodbye to him. I called Jo on the evening of the third day to tell her my flight plans for the return trip to Denver in about ten days. After my call, Robbie left his post and did not return to it until about an hour before Jo went to the airport to pick me up. I should have known he would be psychic!

It was obvious he needed a companion and a backyard to play in, so I bought a house! By the happiest of circumstances, it was directly across the street from the high school in which I taught English and supervised the production of the yearbook for 22 years. South High is a magnificent landmark structure, and in the pictures of its construction in 1924, one can see my little white stucco house, a "hipped roof cottage" designed by Frank Lloyd Wright, with two little maple trees in front. Rob and I went together to look at a litter of Sheltie pups and discovered that their mother was one of the stars in Robbie's obedience class! She had a very fat little boy pup, Elmer, who was already sold, and two girls who were almost identical. I couldn't decide between them, so I brought Robbie in to see if he had a preference, and without a moment's hesitation, he chose Feeny.

This little orange fluff ball was six weeks old when she came to live with us. From the very beginning, Feeny had no interest in me. Clearly, she belonged to Robbie. He slept with one front paw and one back leg flung over her, holding her tightly to keep her in bed. Unlike her hero, Feeny had excellent conformation, and everyone raved about her beautiful color. I was encouraged to show her, but as I had never even been to a dog show, I knew that first I had a lot to learn! I took her to a few fun matches, but I never showed her seriously. She had five litters, but Robbie was never the father. Instead, she was bred to three different local champions. Robbie had no interest at all in breeding her, probably because she had grown up with him, but I had him neutered when he was about five, just to be safe. He thought his pain was unmatched by anything animal or human had ever suffered! He lay in the living room, surrounded by pillows, "enjoying ill health," and I fed him ice chips for days. That finally became boring, and when Feeny came home from being bred, he was ready to go outside to play with her.

Robbie had a very soft, feminine nature, which I first noticed when one of my students brought her litter of Boxer pups over, and Robbie gathered them all to him and tried to nurse them! He was a wonderful help to Feeny, who was the perfect brood bitch but who became distraught when her babies cried, as they did after their dewclaws were removed. Feeny would jump out of the playpen, and Robbie would climb in and scoop the babies under one front paw, where he could lick and kiss each one.

Feeny had many nicknames: "That cute little red-haired girl," "Feeny the Freeloader," because she loved to ride around the yard on the sheet of plastic I used while gardening, and "Miss Lace Britches," because she was so dainty and feminine and always walked around the puddles. My niece, Cathy, affectionately called her "Feenut," and when she was bad, I called her "Fiona," which was part of her registered name, "Argyll's Fionnaghal." In spite of her being so fastidious, Feeny whelped her puppies as if she were "an old fish-wife." Out came the pup, and Feeny grabbed the umbilical cord in her teeth and threw the puppy over her shoulder while she gnawed through the cord, and then cleaned every inch of the baby. She would direct it to the "faucets" and get on with whelping the next one. She was very attached to her babies. When the pups began to go to their new homes, Feeny looked and looked for the first missing pup and then replaced her with a tennis ball. There had been five pups in her first litter, and then there were five tennis balls tucked under her for weeks!

When she wasn't caring for puppies, Feeny was a whiz at obedience school. She started when she was only four months old, and she was at the top of her class until graduation day, when she spotted a friend in the audience and flew into her lap instead of completing the exercise "Come"! She was rarely naughty, but she was very silly and funny! One day when I was at school, a dear friend came over to help clean my yard after a big storm, which had uprooted trees and flooded our basement. Mary put on old clothes and left her regular clothes, including a new bra, on the bed. When I came home, Feeny was running around the house with both front legs through the bra straps!

Unlike Robbie, who was alone with me for his babyhood, Feeny had a lot of human companionship. My cousin Barbara, who is a nurse, moved to Denver and decided to stay with me. She adored the dogs, and spent hours dancing with them! She grew up in Santo Domingo and was an expert at the "Meringue," a noisy dance that the dogs loved. The music was loud, and if Barbara was dancing with Robbie, Feeny barked and barked and ran in circles around them, eager for her turn. Barbara's usual shift at Denver General was from 7 p.m. to 3 a.m., so she was with the dogs all day while I was teaching, and I was there to play with them after school. After we got Feeny, Robbie no longer had a sensitive stomach and became a food stealer! One Sunday afternoon I left a bone-in ham thawing on the kitchen counter and fell asleep watching something on television. When I woke up and went out to put the ham into the oven, I found a bone, a bit of the ham end, and a miserable little black Sheltie. He did a lot of moaning and whining, and he had to lie completely stretched out to relieve his tight, swollen tummy. He did not throw up, nor did he have diarrhea, but that experience taught him a lesson, and it was this: always share what you steal! I had a birthday dinner party for a friend and roasted a leg of lamb with tiny new potatoes. Such heavenly odors wafted from the kitchen late that afternoon! There were four of us at dinner, and each of us ate one slice of the meat. After dinner, we left everything on the table and went out to look at the garden and walk around a bit before dessert. When we came back into the dining room, we saw what little remained of the lamb, and three very pleased dogs — a Kerry Blue terrier, who belonged to one of the guests, and two Shelties. I insisted that Feeny, who was just six months old, was too small to have had a part in the thievery, but her breath smelled of roast lamb, so she had definitely eaten her share!

When Barbara left for a new job in Florida, she took with her Argyll's Morna Meghan, one of Feeny's puppies. Barb didn't miss us nearly as much as we missed her! Oh, how I hated living alone! My friend Vi Cook, who was the secretary at South High by day and an instrumental music teacher most evenings, lived in a small but elegant apartment. She had a new Miniature Poodle puppy who needed friends to play with while she was at work, so each morning, she put him in my backyard, and he grew up thinking he was a Sheltie. It finally occurred to us that Vi and Mr. Bojangles, the dancing Poodle, should leave the apartment and live here. It was a completely satisfactory solution to many problems. My dogs — I had several Shelties by then — adored Vi, and one of them, Nighean, welcomed her by eating her loafers. She started with the tassels, and they were so tasty she finished off the entire instep. I had not yet registered her, so when I did, I made Vi her co-owner. When the registration slip arrived, she ate Vi's clutter boots! Whenever there were thunderstorms or fireworks, the dogs always became frightened and performed certain rituals. Robbie hid behind the furnace, and Feeny looked for Vi. At night on the 4th of July, when neighbor kids shot off their strings of "lady fingers," Feeny would dash into Vi's bedroom and lie on Vi's stomach, panting in her face. I was such a sound sleeper she knew it would be useless to get into my bed! Vi enjoyed reading during the rare times she was at home, and Feeny couldn't stand it. She would race into Vi's study and jump into her lap, landing squarely in the middle of the book.

Feeny's most noted silliness, however, was something she used to do every evening after dinner. She would find a toy and then scurry across the kitchen tile floor with her little toenails clickety clacking. She would stop momentarily in the doorway. And then, as if on the count of three, she would *tear* into the dining room with the toy in her mouth, holding her head high. She would rush past Robbie and fly around the living room and back into the kitchen. If Robbie got up to play, that was the end of her performance. Otherwise, she would repeat her tease until he finally played with her, or she just became fed up with him. We always celebrated birthdays with a little hamburger that had an appropriate number of candles on it. When Robbie was two, he sat politely with his hamburger in front of him, waiting for me to take his picture and give him permission to eat. Feeny waited as long as she could while I fumbled with the camera, and finally she jumped up and snatched the hamburger. Robbie's face was filled with a look of total shock and disbelief. He continued to sit in the chair, looking at the empty plate. You could almost see the tears running down his face. Sometimes, instead of having the hamburger, we went out for ice cream.

Robbie and Feeny lived together in the same house for nine years. The house is situated on a rather quiet street, with the school on the east and a large park with two lakes on the north. Whenever we left the house, the dogs would run out the front door, down the steps, and around to our car in the driveway. It was a path they had followed hundreds of times. On Robbie's tenth birthday, he carried a card from his friend Sally in his mouth all day long. When we walked out the front door to go for his special treat, he did something he had never done in all his life. He saw a jogger across the street in Washington Park, and instead of going around to the car, he ran toward the man so fast that no one could have stopped him — right into a line of Saturday evening traffic speeding along Louisiana Avenue. The cars that hit him did not stop. Vi wrapped him in a towel and carried him to the front porch, where I sat, screaming. Someone brought Feeny to say goodbye. She was waiting next to the car, where he should have been, too.

We buried Robbie in the backyard. I couldn't bear to have anyone take him farther than that away from me. Vi dug his grave in a small stand of aspen trees, and we marked it with a special piece of Colorado marble, and planted white alyssum and blue forget-me-nots around it. Letters and cards of sympathy came from all his friends, who reminisced about the joy he had brought into their lives, what a little "gentleman" he always was, what a pleasure it was to have known him. There were so many messages from my students, fellow teachers, and friends that I filled a scrapbook with them.

Feeny had seen Robbie's body on the porch, and had looked at it and then at me questioningly. A few days later, she began to chew her feet so badly we had to put bandages and then little socks on her. And although she had always been a clown, she brought to an abrupt halt her favorite games and antics such as racing through the house and dumping wastebaskets along the way. We kept two pups from her last litter, Briggie and Piper. She devoted herself completely to Piper, never ceasing to clean her ears and discipline her when the dogs played outside. We were busy at the dog shows with Briggie one weekend when Feeny met us at the door as we returned home. I noticed that she looked fat, but she had always been very trim, and I knew immediately there was something wrong. When I tried to pick her up, I could hardly lift her!

The next day I took her to the vet, who said the weight was really water retention, and that he suspected she had cancer. Not wanting to put her down, I made a deal with the vet. He would operate on her, and if he found widespread cancer, he wasn't to let her wake up. Her last evening at home happened to be St. Patrick's Day, and I invited her special friends to dinner. Feeny was allowed to eat all the corned beef she wanted. When I left her for surgery, I kissed her goodbye, knowing in my heart that she would not be coming home.

They were gone from my life, and it was almost unbearable. These were the two little rascals who got out of the car through an open window and came trailing into church to find me; they were the two who threw back their heads and *howled* whenever I left them in the car! They were the two who knew when we turned a certain corner that we were going to the vet and took it as their cue to begin jumping from the backseat to the front seat and back again, barking wildly; they recognized the purple and white school colors that I wore on Fridays, when the faculty met at a restaurant for breakfast, and they came along for a bit of pancake; they were the ones who waited for me to come home from school, sitting on the back of the couch and watching through the big front window. Now they were gone, and a part of my heart died with them.

I had never considered their coming back from the dead. No one spoke about the "Rainbow Bridge" in those days, and I was not looking forward to apparitions or significant dreams. Robbie had always slept with me in my twin bed. I slept on my right side, and he would curl up spoon-fashion behind me and be as close as he could get. A few nights after he was killed, I was lying in bed, crying, when suddenly there was a bump, followed by a warm feeling along my back. It felt exactly as if Robbie were lying behind me as usual! My first thought was that someone had come to sit on the bed, but when I looked, no one was there! I moved my hand over the area of the bed beside me, and it felt warm. The covers seemed flat, as if someone had been sitting on them. The same sensation occurred frequently after that, especially when I felt really blue. The visitations continued from time to time over the next few years, growing farther and farther apart, and then stopping altogether. I didn't mention his visits to anyone else for a long time. I believed Robbie was telling me that he would never really leave me, that he would always be mine. After each incident, I felt comforted, but there was always a renewed sense of sadness. Our relationship had been so close. Perhaps he visited me because he was as sad to leave me, as I was to lose him. I continued to sleep in that bed until back problems forced me to sleep in a recliner. Since then, I have not felt Robbie's presence.

Feeny was a fun-loving clown in life, and even after "crossing over," she apparently still enjoys a good prank. Many times over the past 24 years, I have caught a fleeting glimpse of her bright orange coat as she streaks past me. I usually see the "orange flash" if I turn my head quickly or look up suddenly from my desk. Often I will find a wastebasket tipped over. I am not the only one who sees her. Vi has had similar experiences. She sees the same orange flash and finds her wastebasket emptied, too. Because I am not the only one who sees her, I am certain that Feeny still lives with us.

When I was a kid, my faith was hard to shake. I believed in Santa Claus and the tooth fairy long, long after I should have known better. As I grew older, though, I first became a skeptic, and finally a devout believer in the soul and in an afterlife. No less a personage than a retired Archbishop of Canterbury once said that the Christian vision of Heaven did not include canines, but this is not an article of faith, and I choose to disagree with him. St. Paul wrote to the Hebrews, "Faith is the realization of what is hoped for and evidence of things not seen." What more could I hope for than a Heaven with my dogs in it — and what evidence more must I have that they are already there waiting for me?

> "I think not how sad that you are gone, but rather how empty it would have been had you never come."
>
> …author unknown

Yukon

...a beautiful Malamute-Samoyed mix dog who lived happily for 16 years with Jayne, a mail carrier in Wisconsin.

I had always wanted a dog, but my mom wouldn't let me have one, fearing that I wouldn't take care of it. Typical Mom! But when I turned 18 and was on my own, we both knew I would be looking for my long-awaited canine companion. The dog of my dreams was born in the backyard of the duplex where I was living. My neighbor had a litter of Malamute-Samoyed mix puppies, and every day I went to see them. From the first visit, I knew there was one that was special, a darker-colored female who was very responsive to me. A special connection grew between us, and I named my new dog "Yukon."

Yukon grew to be very large, and she resembled a wolf, which often intimidated the neighborhood kids. Despite her appearance, however, she was tranquil, sweet, gentle, and affectionate, always greeting everyone with a canine grin. Because of her heavy coat, Yukon could not stay indoors, so I arranged to be outside with her as much as possible. I would drink my coffee outside in the morning, just to be with her. Even when it was very cold and snowy, I'd bundle up with a scarf and heavy coat and sit outside for hours, petting Yukon and thinking how it would be impossible to love anything or anybody more than I loved her. At last I had my perfect dog. I lived for her, and she lived for me. Even my previously dubious mom adored Yukon and had to admit that I was doing a good job taking care of her.

Yukon and I liked to go hiking. As we walked in the fields of tall grass, we loved playing a game of hide and seek. I would slow down just enough to allow Yukon to run ahead of me. Then I would lie down quickly and hide in the grass. Yukon would come back, running, panting, trying to find me, and when she did, I would giggle and hug her and tell her what a clever girl she was. What wonderful, happy times we had! When I think of being with her again, I always picture us on a cool morning, hiking through the tall grass, just as we did before.

Yukon remained healthy for a long time but, sadly, could not go on forever. At 16 she was failing in many ways. Finally she let me know it was time to say farewell. I took her to the veterinary emergency room and stayed with her during the euthanasia process. Afterward, I lay down on the floor next to her and sobbed uncontrollably.

My grief was so intense I was inconsolable. Because I couldn't stop crying, I couldn't go to work. For three days, I literally had my head buried in a pillow, weeping constantly. I felt empty, and my sadness was so profound it was an effort for me to breathe. When I was awake, I merely went through the motions of life; when I slept, I know that I cried, because my face was always wet when I awoke.

On the third day after Yukon died, I was taking a shower, not really thinking about anything but just feeling numb. The soothing water was hitting the back of my neck, and my eyes were closed. Suddenly, I felt a surge of energy rippling down the front of my body. It was a powerful force that traveled from the top of my head to my feet, and it nearly knocked me off balance! Instinctively, I knew it was Yukon. There was no doubt it was my beloved friend. I cried out her name. Smiling for the first time since her death, I opened my eyes. "Wow," I thought. "Yukon just came and poured herself into me!" It sounds eerie, I know, but that was my first thought about what had occurred. I was the pitcher and she was the liquid. I was the glass and she was the water. It felt as if her soul had joined mine! Then, momentarily, I began to doubt the entire episode. "This is too weird," I resolved. "This could not have happened. It's almost like a UFO experience!" But in the next instant, I chastised myself. "Why am I starting to doubt? What I experienced was *real*! How can I tell myself it *didn't* happen when I know it did?"

As soon as I banished my doubts and accepted the reality of the experience, I felt euphoric. I ran out of the bathroom to tell my husband what had happened. He smiled indulgently, but I was sure he didn't believe my story. Remarkably, my intense, debilitating grief was gone. I don't know how I would have overcome it without this experience. I still missed Yukon, of course, but now I was comforted knowing that she was with me and that we would always be together.

I have a few tangible reminders of her. She always had — and shed — a lot of hair! I had some of it spun into yarn and knit into a sweater. Because it is too warm to wear, I keep it on a hanger in the basement, and when I see it, or if I just hold it for a few minutes, it brings back thoughts of her. Sometimes I get butterflies in my stomach and then the tears come, even though I don't usually cry so easily. At other times it makes me feel warm and happy, and I smile remembering the wonderful life and powerful reunion I had with my perfect dog.

Kusak

...a dearly loved Shih Tzu who lived almost 13 years in Cheyenne, Wyoming, with Charlie Esch, a retired interpreter for the deaf.

Some time ago, I was in my yard cleaning up after the dogs when a man walked by and commented on what I was doing. "That's the reason why I'll never own a dog," he remarked. My response was straightforward. "Sir, I am so sorry for you, because you will never experience true, unconditional love." The man mumbled something and continued walking, clearly without a clue as to what I meant.

My first experience with unconditional love came to me in the form of a little Shih Tzu named Kusak. My wife and I bought our first mobile home from a young couple that was moving to attend the University of Wyoming, and since dogs weren't allowed at the university, the couple's two-year-old Shih Tzu became part of the deal. Words cannot express my joy as I held Kusak for the first time. I loved him immediately, and so did my wife. Our adventuresome new life of traveling around the United States began with Kusak as our constant companion. He loved to travel, and usually became the center of attention wherever we went.

Once when we were at a softball game, Kusak jumped into an empty baby stroller. The mother was standing by, holding her infant, not realizing that the baby's stroller had been taken over by a dog! There was Kusak, just sitting and looking around as if the carriage belonged to him. After that, I bought him his own stroller, and took him along in it wherever I went, even into all the stores. I guess we were quite a sight, because we had our picture taken many times. One time we made the front page in Vallejo, California. The headline over our picture read, "Just doggin' it." Another year, I pushed him across the Golden Gate Bridge in his stroller, which caused the maintenance crew to make a big fuss over him. The next year, when the crew saw us coming, one man remarked, "Here comes that lazy little dog again!" And once while I waited on a street corner in San Francisco, a little kid yelled, "Cute dog, mister — but he sure is an ugly baby!"

Our happy life with Kusak continued until he was about ten, when he developed a limp in his left front leg. After several trips to the doctor, a biopsy revealed the sad news that Kusak had cancer. In order to remove the entire tumor, his leg had to be amputated. I felt distraught and cried, but Kusak adapted very well. Thank goodness for that stroller, because now he was still able to go with us wherever we went.

We enjoyed a little more time together until Kusak's general health deteriorated and his heart enlarged. I decided to take him to a cardiac specialist about a hundred miles from where I was living. The vet examined him and wanted to keep him overnight. The following morning as I was about to return to the hospital, the phone rang. It was the vet, informing me that Kusak had had a heart attack during the night, and was dead! Imagine how devastated and shocked I felt. That day, I drove back home with Kusak's body in a box next to me. What a terrible, long trip it was! I cried and talked to my little dog constantly as if he were still alive.

The night after I brought Kusak home, I was in bed, trying to sleep. I was lying there in the dark with my eyes wide open, when suddenly I saw Kusak running back and forth across a green meadow! It was a beautiful field, and it reminded me of the scene described in the poem, "The Rainbow Bridge." Kusak appeared healthy and happy as he scampered around on four strong legs. At one point, he stopped running and looked straight at me. What a special moment that was! Then he ran away to play with a German Shepherd, who must have been his old friend Charlie, who had passed away a year earlier. Charlie belonged to my youngest daughter, and whenever we visited my daughter, Charlie and Kusak would always play together. After Charlie died, Kusak repeatedly searched every room for him. It broke my heart to see him missing his friend so much. To console him, I would pick up my little guy and explain that Charlie had gone to the Rainbow Bridge and that one day, he would see him again. Some people would say I'm nuts to talk to a dog like that, but who cares? How great it is to be nuts and to share such love!

My vision of Kusak lasted only about 30 seconds. Since then, there have been other more subtle contacts.

Sometimes I get a fleeting glimpse of him or sense his presence. Occasionally, I've felt his weight on me as though he were sitting on my lap. I still feel the loss, and the hurt never goes away completely, but the vision of him running in the open meadow and playing with Charlie continues to comfort me and bring me great joy. Now I know where Kusak is, and I believe that I will see him again some day.

To be honest, I really wasn't surprised to see Kusak that night, because some years earlier, I had seen my deceased father in a vision. I suppose that most people wonder, after a loved one dies, if that person still has a human form, and if he has gone to Heaven, wherever that is. I missed my father so I had those questions, and often wondered if I would see him again. Then one day as I was looking out the window, I saw his face, surrounded by a cloud! He seemed to be looking down at me from the sky. After that experience, I felt peaceful and knew that my questions had been answered.

Gigio

...a dog, probably a mixture of German Shepherd and Pit Bull, who spent ten wonderful years with Ana Maria Bueno, a salesperson.

Gigio came into my life when I was going to college in Florida. At the time, I wanted a dog desperately, but I couldn't afford to buy one. The breed didn't matter. I just kept saying, "If someone would give me a dog — any dog — I would take it!" My wish came true when a close friend of mine happened upon a litter of puppies that were being given away outside a shopping mall. Knowing how much I wanted a dog, he picked one out and gave him to me. What a happy day that was!

If you are old enough to remember the Beatles' appearances on the Ed Sullivan Show, you'll remember the little mouse puppet, Topo Gigio. My sister decided the perfect name for the puppy was Gigio, as he was so small I could put him into my pocket, and he had little "mouse" ears! I'm sure my puppy was too young to leave his mother, but the person who raised the litter must have been tired of the whole thing, and just took the babies to the mall to give them away, with little regard for the quality of the new homes. Gigio was also — how can I put it kindly — a very ugly dog, probably the result of the strange mixture that went into his breeding. At the time, I had no idea what that breeding might have included. I didn't care. I had my dog, and nothing else mattered.

Much to my surprise, Gigio grew to be gorgeous and very large. He was also smart, funny, crazy, and totally loving. Later, I decided he was a mixture of German Shepherd and Pit Bull, and in spite of that questionable heritage, he had a gentle disposition and would never have hurt any living thing. Needless to say, he brought me much happiness at a time when I was going through a difficult transition. I was living away from my family — and a longtime pampered existence — for the first time. My sister and I had a small, gloomy, cockroach-infested apartment, and both of us were struggling financially. Thank goodness for Gigio! He was my reason to get up in the morning, to keep going. He needed me.

What a rambunctious dog he was. His greatest delight was getting us to chase him. To initiate the chase game, he would steal a pillow or a shoe or some clothing that he should not have, and then go racing and tearing through the apartment. My sister and I would run after him, trying to catch him to retrieve the pilfered item. The faster we chased and the louder we screamed, the more he loved it! When one of us managed to tackle him and grab his treasure, we would all collapse in a heap, laughing, and Gigio would have a big smile on his face.

One night my sister and I went out for dinner and left our young Gigio alone in the apartment. That was a *big* mistake. When we returned, we discovered that he had ransacked my sister's closet, and had chewed either one shoe or both from each pair of shoes, leaving her with none to wear except for those she had on. It is funny to look back at this destruction, but it wasn't quite so funny when it happened.

For half of his life, Gigio lived in apartments. Even though dogs were allowed wherever we lived, we always tried to hide our "brute," especially from the apartment manager, because Gigio looked like a mean Pit Bull, and "Pit Bull panic" had infected our state. Inevitably, Gigio would get out and find the manager, who would be frightened as soon as he saw our large, ferocious-looking animal. As the manager was beating a hasty retreat, Gigio would begin to chase him, thinking that this was just another version of his favorite game. We would receive an eviction notice within a day or two. Over a period of five years, we moved at least six times! Gigio had acquired an undeservedly bad reputation — he loved everything and everyone and was never aggressive. He even tolerated my pet mice!

It took five years, but we finally moved into a house. We taught Gigio to bring in the newspaper, and he loved to do it, but unfortunately, he could not distinguish our newspaper from that of our neighbor. We should have known he would pick up the neighbor's paper, too. When we tried to get the paper away from him, the chase game would begin and the newspaper would end up as confetti!

When Gigio was ten, I noticed that there was something wrong with him, and instinctively sensed it was life-threatening. The vet who examined him thought otherwise, however, and dismissed the symptoms as "nothing important." Two weeks later, a remarkable event occurred. Ray and I were living together at the time, and our bedroom had three large, uncovered windows that let in the moonlight and starlight so that the room was never really dark. Ray awoke in the middle of the night to see a white, transparent lady bending toward Gigio, who was asleep on the floor next to the bed. The lady caressed and stroked Gigio while he sighed. "As quickly as the lady appeared," Ray said, "she disappeared."

After the vision, Gigio appeared to be getting worse, so we took him back to the vet. This time, they found that his body was filled with inoperable cancer. We stayed with Gigio as he was put to sleep.

For many years, I had meditated in bed at night, and I continued to do so after Gigio died. About two weeks after his death, I found the pain of missing him became almost unbearable; as I lay there, trying to relax, I kept wishing that I could touch him and pet him one more time. I prayed for ten or fifteen minutes, and suddenly, *there he was*! His face was next to mine, and his body was stretched out on top of me. Alive, he had been a heavy dog, but now he felt very light. He looked at me and I could see his eyes. He started to lick my face as I stroked him. His body felt just as I remembered. This wonderful exchange of my petting him and his kissing my face continued for several precious minutes. Then he was gone. Believing that most people would dismiss my experience as a dream or the product of my vivid imagination, I told only a few close friends about it. But I know what I saw. I know what I felt. I know it was real!

Two or three days later, Ray and I were watching television in the evening, when the scent of flowers suddenly filled the room. It was as if we were in a field of roses. We looked knowingly at each other; there was no need for words. It was obvious we both smelled the scent and believed it was from Gigio. The sweet aroma lasted only a few minutes. I have never smelled that fragrance before or since that time.

I feel sad for those who think that life ends when we die. My experience with Gigio has made it easier for me to say goodbye to those who leave, whether they are human beings or animals. Gigio's visitation confirmed my belief that animals have souls and that they, as well as people, continue in some form of existence after death.

Six Pack *plus* One

...seven Huskies who loved two adventurous photographers, Greg Barrett and Dave Wohlenberg, and lived for their frequent forays into the Alaskan wilderness. The "six-pack plus one" consisted of Trax, who lived to be almost 13, Chika, almost 11, Quest and Kristy, both 15, Kozie, almost 10, Smokey, 14, and Happy, 13 years old, and still alive when this story was written.

My name is Greg Barrett, and as a young man, I moved from Iowa to Alaska in 1980 to live an adventuresome life in the wilderness. For several years, I lived alone, until I got my first two dogs, Trax and Chica, two six-week-old Husky-Shepherd mix puppies. My friend Dave Wohlenberg, who came to live in Alaska in 1985, eventually got two Huskies, Quest and Kristy. In 1988, he bought a remote five-acre parcel of land, and there in the midst of the trees, we built two separate hillside cabins. Several years later, my dog Trax mated with Dave's dog Kristy, creating a litter of six puppies. Dave kept one pup, Smokey, and I kept Kozie. The remaining pups went to other homes.

With that, Dave and I had three dogs and one cabin each. Things changed in a few years when Dave had to return to a full-time job. He was still home many evenings and most weekends, but out of necessity and concern for his three dogs, Dave agreed that they should live with me, although he would visit them regularly. So it came to be that six large dogs and I lived together in my small but adequate cabin.

This Husky group formed the "six-pack" who climbed the mountains, swam the lakes and rivers, and chased the squirrels. They became my remote sensors in every wilderness adventure. I was just another member of the pack and took the dogs wherever I went, whenever it was possible. The dogs never wore collars, nor were they restrained in any way. The bond that grew between us was stronger than any human bond I'd ever experienced. To say we were close would be an understatement. I never felt happier than when I was with these dogs.

Each member of the six-pack had a distinct personality. Trax was the dignified king who always lay down with his paws crossed. When Dave or I patted him, he made "love grunts." Chika was the queen. She and I shared such closeness that I felt we were one soul. Kozie liked to stand on her hind legs. Quest, who lived the longest, was always happy. Kristy loved to chase squirrels, and because she could say one discernible word — "rub" — we often called her "Rubbie." Smokey was noted for her characteristic howl that sounded like a Lionel train whistle.

Here's The Rub

Chika was the first dog to pass away. She had been ill with lymphosarcoma and died shortly after surgery at the veterinary clinic. I was shocked when I got the news. Her passing hit me hard because I had been so close to her, and this was my first encounter with death. I brought her body home and placed it outside in a coffin, some distance from my cabin, planning to bury her the next day.

That evening, Smokey behaved in a most unusual manner. She sat and stared into the woods where Chika's coffin was lying. She barked continuously, and turned her head back and forth as if she were watching something move — something I couldn't see! The next morning, Trax also barked for a long time for no apparent reason, which was totally out of character for him. Like Smokey, he also turned his head as if he were looking at something that was moving.

The day I buried Chika, I couldn't bear to stay home. Dave had some time off, so we took a long ride with the dogs in order to get away for a while. As we returned home, we saw a vivid, breathtaking rainbow, which appeared to extend from my cabin across to another part of the hill, where a musher lived. I was to learn later that it was much more than just a beautiful arc of color in the sky.

It was winter, and exactly five months after the day we saw the rainbow. The snowfall had been unusually heavy, so Dave and I went out to plow the road leading from his cabin to the highway. About halfway down the hill, we saw a young Husky in the middle of the road, alone and seemingly lost. We stopped, but as soon as we did, she scampered into the woods. I called out to her, and ever so cautiously she approached as I continued to coax her gently to come closer. Eventually I was able to reach out and pet her. Then I let her go, but instead of running away, she followed us. I finally put her into the truck and took her home. Back at the cabin, my Husky visitor surprised me by running upstairs and jumping immediately onto my bed. She seemed to be

familiar with my cabin, as if she had been there before! Her behavior reminded me so much of Chika that I remember thinking, "If this isn't an example of reincarnation, I don't know what is."

The possibility of reincarnation was strengthened further when I finally found her owner. He was the musher who lived at the other end of the rainbow that Dave and I had seen exactly five months ago. Later I learned my new Husky had been born on the day of the rainbow. It gave me chills when I realized that the rainbow had magically connected my cabin to the musher's cabin where the pup had been born. After some finagling, the young dog became mine. I named her "Happy." She was readily accepted to join the "six-pack" and became the "plus one."

Two years after Chika died, her brother Trax passed away at home one night while I was sleeping. Like Chika, he had developed lymphosarcoma. Not long afterward, I heard whining noises on several occasions, even though no dogs were near. A few times, the newspaper fell off the couch for no apparent reason; but the most amazing thing was a mystical white cloud that appeared suddenly outside my bedroom window.

I always like to lie in bed and look out my large window into the forest before falling asleep. One night, some months after Trax's passing, I was startled to see a cloud or misty ring hovering around a nearby tree. "What on earth is that?" I wondered, sitting up in bed, and now wide-awake. I began to have an eerie feeling, as if I were watching a spooky movie. The apparition was about eight feet from where I was sitting in bed. It moved and swirled, changing its form. Sometimes it formed a crude, circular pattern, probably a foot thick and about ten feet in diameter. The ghostly mist appeared nightly for a few weeks, usually remaining for half an hour, and then it abruptly disappeared.

The first time I watched the mist, I was astonished by what I saw. My feelings gradually changed to awe, as I came to believe that I was seeing the spirits of my deceased dogs, Trax and Chika. I often wanted to photograph the phenomenon, but there was never enough light.

As the years went by, Dave and I experienced the loss of all our dogs except Happy. Then Dave happened to read about some spooky phenomena that had occurred at Angels Rest Pet Memorial Park in Utah. Apparently some visitors at the park had taken pictures of the gravesites, and unexplained cloudy images appeared in the photos, similar to what I had observed from my bedroom window. Out of curiosity, Dave decided to photograph our dogs' gravesites.

When we got the photos back, we were shocked to see a ghostly cloud around the graves of Kozie, Quest, and Kristy. The misty image reminded me of what I had seen night after night, and convinced me that I had truly been looking at the spirits of the dogs! The hovering mist only appeared in one of the photos, gravesites or otherwise. Incidentally, I had previously taken pictures and videos of our dogs' graves and had never seen the  apparition that appeared in Dave's photos. Of course, the mist seen in the photo was not visible to the naked eye the day the picture was taken. I want to stress that this story and the photo *are not a hoax*. The dogs meant everything to me. It would be disrespectful to my "best friends" if this were made up.

I've described the larger paranormal events, but smaller incidents also occurred that I think are worth mentioning. Whenever one of the dogs passed away, there was a rainbow, a beautiful sunset, or a spectacular Northern Lights show. Occasionally, I felt unexplained movements on my bed, and sometimes, while sitting at a table, I would put my foot down and swear I sensed a tail or paw, only to look down and see nothing. My friend Dave confessed that he heard Smokey bark shortly after the dog passed away.

As a result of my experiences, I have come to believe that there is a different "plane of existence." The souls of the dogs are like energy or radio waves, and sometimes I am lucky enough to be aware of them. I trust that one day I will be in their realm and be reunited with them. My dogs are waiting for me to join them, probably preparing "a special dog house" for me. My newly discovered beliefs have given me comfort, but for now, I must remain on this earthly plane with my only dog, Happy. As I write this, she is approaching 13. When the time is right, I hope to adopt more dogs to keep me company.

I made a promise to my dogs that I would never forget them. Honoring and memorializing them in this book helps. Their names are engraved on bronze plaques, displayed in a park dedicated to Fairbanks's first family. Their plaques will be there forever, just as the memories of them are forever in my heart. Close to my cabin and the dogs' gravesites, I have nailed a special wooden plaque to a tree. Engraved on it is a line from the song, *"Suddenly Last Summer,"* which says it all:

Speeder

...a playful little Cairn Terrier who spent his 15 years with Marsha J. West and some animal friends in Texas. Marsha loves Tai Chi and studying veterinary medicine.

My Cairn Terrier Speeder was quite an athlete, and whether the toy was a Frisbee, a tugger, or a ball, he was ready for a game. One of his favorite toys was a big plastic ball, which was kept inside. He would play by himself for hours, pushing, kicking, bouncing, and chasing the ball all over the house. It didn't take much encouragement to get the little jock involved in a game with me, either. All I had to say was, "Come on, Speeder! Get your ball!" and he was ready to play. Once the game began, he insisted on our playing for a long time. What a joy seeing him have so much fun!

Speeder's zest for life showed up in full force when it snowed. He loved the stuff, and couldn't wait to run outside, where he would burrow into the cold, white powder and emerge completely covered by it. His playfulness continued as he rolled and ate the snow. Speeder and I spent many happy hours playing in the snow with his special ball or Frisbee. I would throw the toy and he would leap exuberantly, chase after it, and bring it back to me. If I didn't throw it faster and faster, he would get mad and tell me off!

I was Speeder's favorite person, but that didn't stop him from adoring other people and animals, especially horses. Speeder saw horses for the first time on television. He watched intently as they ran across the screen. Once they had disappeared, he ran to the back door, expecting them to show up in his backyard. He was quite mystified when they weren't there! His love affair with horses continued throughout his life. Every Sunday we would take him for a ride to a country farm, where we knew there were horses. As soon as one came into view, Speeder would whine, bark, and jump at the window. We would stop the car and I would carry a very excited little dog to the fence for a closer look. At first the horses were frightened and stayed away, but gradually they got used to him and even came running when they saw us approaching. Of course Speeder was delighted! I was always so touched to see him and the horses together. My little terrier would lick their noses as the horses pushed their big heads into his face and neck.

One thing Speeder didn't like was swimming or getting wet. For that reason, he absolutely detested our pool and hid every time we put on our bathing suits. In spite of his protesting, I put Speeder into the pool once a year to reacquaint him with the location of the stairs so that if he fell into the water, he would know how to get out. On one particular occasion, the weather was quite hot, and Speeder had just endured his yearly visit to the pool. Afterward, I placed him on a big blue float and let him "tour" the pool. He sat calmly and thoroughly enjoyed himself now that he was safe and getting dry. He had no idea how hilarious he looked — just like a big, drowned rat. The scene was so comical that I took his picture and submitted it to *Dog World* magazine. They loved the photo and one summer published it as their centerfold!

When Speeder was about 13, he was diagnosed with a herniated disc in his neck. The vet refused to do surgery because he felt that Speeder was not in pain, but I knew better. Speeder was a stoic little dog who hid his feelings well. To get additional opinions, I took him to several other vets. About six months later, Speeder underwent surgery, but by that time, his spinal cord had been damaged beyond repair and he was crippled. His health continued to deteriorate, and before long, he was partially paralyzed and needed a lot of personal care. I believe the recent deaths of two of his buddies, our cat, Chaucer, and our other dog, Margaret, contributed to his unwillingness to get better. Speeder had been especially close to Margaret, who was also a Cairn Terrier. Every night, I used to tell Speeder that it would be okay for him to go to heaven because Chaucer and Margaret were already there. Finally an ultrasound showed that Speeder had numerous systemic problems. As I pondered what to do, he turned and looked at me hopefully. "Do you mind if I go?" his eyes seemed to ask. I told him quietly, "No, Baby Boy, I don't mind." Speeder sighed and was at peace. He was euthanized on March 5, 2003.

Several months later, I was sitting, wide awake, on the sofa. Out of nowhere, a vision of Speeder appeared spontaneously in front of me. I hadn't even been thinking of him, and yet, suddenly, he was there. What I saw was like a movie, appearing real and three-dimensional. My precious little dog, no longer crippled or in pain, was running happily, with his long hair flying. Along with Speeder were his feline friend, Chaucer and his special, lifetime companion, Margaret. Chaucer had his paws wrapped around Speeder's neck and looked like Superman's cape as he hung onto him. Little Margaret, with her short legs, was running as fast as she could beside her old friend, trying her best to keep up with him. She was nipping at Speeder's side, trying to make him slow down. They had often run together exactly like that when they were alive. The colors were vivid, from the animals' hair to the tall, green grass and deep blue sky with fluffy, white clouds. There was even a slight breeze blowing. It seemed as if time stood still, and I was aware of nothing else. The vision probably lasted only a few seconds, but I felt its effects for many weeks. I sobbed as it faded, knowing that Speeder had come to show me that he was happy, that he could run and play again, and that he had been reunited with Chaucer and Margaret. I have never forgotten the experience.

Another significant visitation from Speeder occurred when I was in the kitchen one evening. I was feeling very blue and crying when I suddenly sensed his presence. I looked to my right and saw him sitting next to me. Once again, the vision consumed my total attention. Speeder's head was cocked as he looked up at me. I could see his flowing golden hair and his beautiful brown eyes. He appeared to be healthy and young, probably about four years old. His image was solid rather than transparent. His eyes locked mine, and I felt his love radiating toward me. "Speeder!" I said, and then he was gone. It amazed me to realize that he must have sent a telepathic message to make me sense his arrival. I knew he had come to comfort me, because he was always there to respond to my sadness.

I know that I did not lose Speeder completely when he died. He came back on those two occasions, and I have often sensed his presence, confirming that our loving relationship continues even after death. On the Other Side, he is still aware of me as I am of him. When I die, Speeder's ashes will be joined with mine as a symbol of our everlasting togetherness.

Gypsy

...a miniature long-haired Dachshund who lived for 15 years in Florida with her friend Linda, a promotions director who loves dogs, sports, and travel.

After my little Dachshund passed away in 1998, she returned to contact me in the most extraordinary manner. Although the experience occurred more than six years ago, it remains vivid in my memory as if it happened yesterday. Until now, there were very few people who knew what happened to me.

I got Gypsy when she was only six weeks old. She was a red and black longhaired miniature Dachshund with beautiful, big brown eyes. Her official registered name was Gypsy Rose Von Weiner. She had a wonderfully happy disposition, constantly wagging her tail and making friends wherever she went. Her affectionate kisses were the thing that made her so special to me. She loved to lick my face and hands, especially the palm of my hands. Kissing my hands was without a doubt her favorite thing to do, so naturally I nicknamed her "Mrs. Kisses."

Besides being a sweet dog, she liked a game of "roughhouse," especially when it involved pulling her ears. I would begin the game by getting down on the floor and teasing, "I'm going to get you! You'd better watch out because here I come!" Then I would grab her ears and she always reacted by stepping back so that her ears were being pulled. Sometimes I would hold her ears and lift her front feet off the ground. She loved my tugging at her, and always came back for more, grinning from ear to ear.

Despite being close to the ground and weighing only nine pounds, Gypsy was a skilled and determined hunter. More than once, I found a "gift" when I returned home. The gifts were always strategically placed where I could not miss them! My little dog always looked so proud, as if she were bragging, "Hey, Mom! Look what I brought you." Her gifts included rats, mice, moles, snakes, and birds, especially Blue Jays, which are numerous where I live.

Gypsy had a long and healthy life, but toward the end, she became weak and her appetite began to wane so that I had to feed her by hand. When she seemed almost too feeble to lick my hands, I knew it was time to let her go. Kissing my hand was the last thing she did before she died!

After her death, I went through an extremely tough time. I was heartbroken and in the throes of grief and depression. For at least six months, I drew pictures of Gypsy to ease my sadness and to help me heal. Several of my drawings are included with this story. These are by no means great art, but rather expressions of love and longing for my little girl.

Several months after Gypsy died, I was sleeping when I awoke to feel someone licking my hand! It was just as Gypsy used to do. I felt her warm tongue kissing my palm over and over again. I remained very still and did not open my eyes for fear that the spell would be broken. It was so comforting and soothing that I just wanted to lie in bed and enjoy it. I remember thinking, "Oh, please don't stop. This is so wonderful!" The sensation continued for a minute or so and then gradually grew less and stopped. I opened my eyes then, and could think of nothing except how to bring Gypsy back and to bring back her kisses. It was difficult to go back to sleep, but I finally drifted off, feeling grateful that she had visited me.

I have always believed that animals have souls that exist after death. I have no doubt that Gypsy was with me that night, giving me a clear message of love. I can't make her come back, but my precious memories sustain me. I keep her collar and her ashes in a special place, along with drawings and poems expressing my endless devotion for her.

Smoke

...a Siberian Husky with a coat you wanted to bury your face in, and sky-blue eyes that seemed to see things beyond our sight. He lived in Michigan for 13 years with Pat Wedzel, a nurse.

Normally, I wouldn't believe that dead pets could communicate with their owners. I have a scientific mind, so the idea of afterlife contacts seems creepy and bizarre. But several events occurred after the passing of my Siberian Husky that literally changed the way I view the world.

From the moment I got Smoke in 1990, I loved him. He was a beautiful black-and-white dog with a thick, soft coat and intelligent, clear blue eyes. About the same time I acquired Smoke, I was laid off from work. Misfortune turned into fortune, as now I was able to devote eight wonderful months to my new companion. Never have I bonded so closely with an animal! We did everything together, sleeping, walking, playing, and eating Chinese food. If I was in a bad mood, Smoke consoled me by snuggling next to me or leaning against my leg. He always wanted to be near me and would even rest his head on my shoulder as I drove my car.

Male Huskies are usually quite excitable, but not Smoke. He never pulled on the leash while we were taking our two-mile walks around the neighborhood. People were always fascinated with his good behavior, his beauty, and his small size, weighing only 45 pounds. On several different occasions, people asked if they could buy him. "No," was my emphatic answer, "he isn't for sale!"

When Smoke was five months old, I took him to obedience school. The instructor was amazed at how quickly he learned to heel and sit, and how gentle and well behaved he was. He always listened to me and seemed to understand almost immediately what I wanted. He was literally "the perfect dog."

The end came in 2003, when Smoke was 13. The vet discovered a malignant tumor on Smoke's kidney, and since it appeared not to have metastasized, the vet attempted the difficult surgery to remove it. As he did, however, the tumor ruptured, sending malignant cells all through Smoke's body. There was no point in continuing the surgery. Euthanizing Smoke was the only humane choice. Needless to say, I was a wreck, totally overcome by the sudden loss of my beloved companion.

Two hours after Smoke was euthanized, I was in the kitchen with my other dog, Cinnamon. Smoke was constantly on my mind. As I was remembering how Smoke and I used to eat Chinese food together, I suddenly said aloud to Cinnamon, "We're going to have Chinese food, and that will make us feel better!" As soon as I said this, I heard a noise in the pantry. I opened the door, and there on the floor was Smoke's choke chain! It was the one he had always worn, but on the day he went to the hospital, I had removed it and placed it in a plastic bag on the pantry shelf. Now it seemed to have fallen onto the floor at the exact moment I mentioned Chinese food! The timing was pretty amazing, but I didn't think much about it until hours later, when a second extraordinary event occurred.

Smoke liked to sit behind a particular drape in my living room so that he could look out the window to see if I was coming home. The drapes have weights at the bottom to keep them hanging evenly. As I entered the living room to turn on the television, I heard a noise that sounded like a curtain weight hitting the wall. I turned in the direction of the sound and saw that the drape was moving! The noise and the movement were exactly as they had been when Smoke came out to welcome me! Sensing a presence near me, I uttered, "Oh, my God. Smoke is here, in this room!" Shivers ran all over me, and goose bumps popped out all over my body.

Moments later, my scientific, rational mind caused me to look for a logical explanation. I thought of Cinnamon, but he wasn't in the living room. I checked the furnace, but it wasn't on. I checked the windows. They were closed. Then I recalled that the choke chain had fallen off the pantry shelf just as I was talking about Chinese food. In light of what I had just experienced with the drape, the previous incident now took on a significant meaning. I truly believe that Smoke sensed my sorrow and contacted me to help me deal with my loss. Despite fleeting moments of doubt, I see no other explanation for the events that occurred.

Then a third episode convinced me that Smoke had not left me to grieve alone. When Smoke was a puppy, he loved to chew on rawhide sticks as I held them in my hand. After Smoke died, I rescued a Cocker Spaniel from the pound, and named him Charlie. Unlike Smoke, Charlie never played with or chewed the rawhide toys, but one day while I was crying, he picked up a piece of rawhide from the floor and brought it to me. He placed it on my lap and rested his head against my leg. His actions reminded me so much of Smoke that I was inclined to believe that somehow Smoke had come to visit me again.

Poochie

...a Labrador mix who lived for six short years with Paula Dodge, President of the Pet Retirement Center (www. wildcatranch.net) in Comfort, Texas.

About 40 years ago, a lanky Yellow Lab-mix came to live with us when his original owners could no longer take care of him. We were living in a rural area and had plenty of room for another critter, even though we already had three cats and a dog. The newcomer was young, probably less than two years old, and looked a lot like "Old Yeller." We called him "Poochie."

During the day Poochie stayed outside, but never strayed far from home. Forty years ago, it was customary for people living in the country to allow their dogs to roam. In the evening, Poochie would scratch, whine, and sometimes bark at the door to let us know that he wanted to come inside. Once inside, he would sleep with our other animals in the basement.

What I remember most about Poochie was his sweet, lovable disposition. He would run as fast as he could to greet us whenever we came home. I can picture him now, ears flopping, tail wagging, and tongue hanging out, ready to slobber all over us! Poochie was just a big, lovable guy who didn't have a mean bone in his body. Our house was situated below the public road, so my two girls had to walk up a slope to get to the school bus stop. Every morning, Poochie would tag along. When the girls returned from school, Poochie was always waiting anxiously to greet them. One winter we had such a bad ice storm that the slope was too slippery for the kids to climb. Leave it to my husband, Denny, to come to the rescue. He put on his golf shoes with steel cleats and got a rope. The girls hung onto the rope while my husband pulled them up the slope to the waiting school bus. Poochie, on the other hand, wasn't that lucky. He desperately wanted to follow the girls, but as soon as he started up the slope, his front legs would slip, causing him to fall on his nose. Over and over he tried, but he just couldn't figure out how to make it up that hill. We all had a good laugh, and I imagine that Poochie thought it was pretty funny, too.

Some years later on a Friday evening, Poochie came home seriously injured and dragging one of his hind legs. I was shocked to see that he had been shot by a high-powered rifle. One of our neighbors had such a gun, and he had complained several times about Poochie barking at night. His complaints were never justified because Poochie was *always* inside our house in the evening. Although my family had explained this to the neighbor, I believe he had already decided that our dog was a nuisance and had planned to take revenge. I suspect he shot Poochie, thinking that he had gotten into the deer carcass that was hanging in his yard. I doubt seriously that Poochie was responsible. Two large dogs, Rhodesian Ridgebacks, were running freely in the area, and they were most likely the culprits. As I examined Poochie's wound, I became very angry with my neighbor. "How could anyone do such a terrible thing to this sweet, affectionate dog?" I wondered.

I rushed Poochie to the vet, hoping to save his leg. The damaged leg had to be amputated, but after the surgery, Poochie seemed to do well. On Sunday morning the vet called to report that Poochie was already eating and standing up in his cage. The doctor seemed optimistic about his recovery. I was so relieved, and looked forward to many more years with my big friendly companion.

I got to bed late that Sunday night. As I started to drift off, I suddenly heard whining, scratching, and barking at the door. It sounded exactly like Poochie, wanting to come in. "How could that be?" I wondered. "He's at the hospital, but perhaps the vet dropped him off early." Again I heard the familiar noises. I got out of bed and walked down the hallway to the front door, all the time aware of the scratching, whining, and barking. As soon as I opened the door and looked outside the sounds stopped! Poochie wasn't there! Nothing was there! I was stunned. Now I started to doubt what I had heard. "Probably the wind blowing a tree branch against the house, or just my imagination," I thought, heading back to bed.

Early the next morning, the vet called with shocking news. Poochie had died unexpectedly during the night. When I heard the news, I no longer doubted what I had heard. I knew for certain that Poochie had come to the house the previous night. He had stopped to let me know that he was all right, even though he would no longer be with me in the physical world. Although I felt grateful for Poochie's visit, I was naturally very upset about his death, and even angrier now with the neighbor who had shot him. How senseless and totally unfair that an innocent animal should die in this violent manner! Our neighbor always denied shooting Poochie, but I know better, even though I could never prove it. We buried our "Old Yeller" in our backyard to keep him as close to us as possible.

"The day will come when men such as I will look on the murder of animals as they now look on the murder of men."

....Leonardo da Vinci

Sasha

...a tiny sable and white Shetland Sheepdog who lived only four years with her beloved Hannah, a college student and professional gardener.

Human beings inherit a lot of physical characteristics as well as personality traits from their ancestors. Sometimes the ancestors don't live long enough for us to become acquainted with them, and we never know that our big nose and flat feet are just like our Great Uncle Frank's! In the canine world, with so many generations possible in a short time, one can see the traits and even the markings coming down from great-great-grandmother to puppy. I don't remember whether I read it in a book or magazine, or in a Sheltie club newsletter, but I know that I have been familiar with the term "Blenheim Markings" for a long, long time. Blenheim Spaniels were among the breeds that contributed to the formation of the Shetland Sheepdogs, and the colors and patterns of these spaniels are seen in many Shelties today. The great "foundation bitch" of the generations of Argyll champions, Robin, had them — the egg-shaped mark of white hairs on top of the head, right between the ears, the white blaze, the white ruff, the white "tuxedo" front, and the fluffy white tip on the very end of the tail. New puppies always looked as if their little tails had been dunked in white paint to give them that finishing touch! Robin also had tan markings on her cheeks and eyebrows and in a cross shape just under the base of her tail. Her owners used to call her "Hot Cross Buns"!

Sasha was one of four Sheltie puppies born after my family moved to California. She weighed all of two ounces, and my mom had to rub her little body gently between her palms to keep her warm, and hold her close to Magic, her mother, to eat because she didn't have the strength to do it on her own. She was one of those teeny, tiny Sheltie pups that you just can't part with, so she was bound to stay in the family.

So it was that I, by then 19 years old and a freshman at the University of Colorado, received Sasha "officially" as a Christmas gift in 2001. I had fallen in love with her as soon as I saw her, with her little teddy bear face, her mellow demeanor, and that perfect little blonde coat with the white Argyll "diamond" on the very top of her head, right between her ears...and let's not forget the white on the very tip of her tail! I had moved into my first apartment, all by myself, and Sasha was just what I needed to overcome the loneliness. I remember holding my tiny girl when I flew back to Colorado. Later, I discovered that she loved to curl up in the small of my back to sleep in the nighttime, and she loved to hike, eat snow, and blow bubbles in her water dish.

After that first year of college, my friend Eric and I decided to wander westward, without any particular destination. I left almost everything in my apartment in Boulder, and we were off on a new adventure, traveling, camping around, and thinking of settling down in California if we could find the right place to make a permanent home. Sasha loved riding in the car and sleeping under the stars. She was the "Queen" of our family, our sweet little angel. It took some searching, but finally, there it was — our house. It needed a lot of repairs, but it was on several acres of good farmland, and it was close to my mother. In addition to renovating the house, we were interested in professional gardening. We spent most of the sunny days working in the yard. Sasha loved to lie in the shade and watch us work in the garden. When she was excited, she would run figure eights around the yard as fast as she could go. She loved to smell the newly mown grass, and to stick her little Sheltie nose into the flowers and sniff deeply. She looked like a hummingbird gathering nectar!

When Sasha was three, we brought home an addition to the family — a German Shepherd-Heeler-Coyote mix puppy. Althea and Sasha became like sisters who loved each other. They would play in the yard and on the sofa, lick faces and sing together... until the day when, without warning, Sasha's life ended, and Eric and I felt that our whole world had ended, too.

I had gone home for the day to see what was going on "down on the farm," where there was always a new horse, or perhaps a newly rescued dog. People tended to dump unwanted pets on or near where my softhearted mother would pick them up and nurse them back to health. As she could not bear to part with them after she got to know them, the menagerie grew and grew! Eric was working in the garden and had run a couple of errands in the car, taking Sasha along as we always did. Sasha stayed in the car while Eric ran his last errand, delivering something to the home of a friend. He had trouble with the gate latch and was just out of Sasha's view, taking far more time than she expected. She was in a hurry to go again, to get that car moving. Sasha stretched her little body to look out of the car window, and she went just a few inches too far and fell out, landing on her neck and breaking it. She died instantly, which was the only good thing we could think about it. It nearly killed Eric to call me with the news.

I rushed back home, but nothing seemed to matter anymore. Hadn't the world ended? What was the point of going on? Our hearts were broken, and sadness had struck us in a way we had never felt before, or ever knew it was possible to feel. Althea would not sing or talk. That had always been her favorite thing to do.

A few days after the accident, I was thinking about Sasha and wishing she were here in the crook of my arm, when I suddenly felt her spirit enter my heart! I looked down at my arm, and there was one long, white hair growing — just one! I knew then she would be with me forever. Later that evening, I was petting Althea, who had always been a solid color of brown with a black stripe down her back, and I was surprised to see a few small white hairs sprouting out of the very tip of her tail! Sasha wanted us to know she was still watching over us. My mother called a few days later to see how we were getting along, and she told me the strangest thing had happened. Her little yellow dog, a rescued Terrier mix she called Muffin, had sprouted a ring of white hairs on the very top of her golden head, right between the ears! And the cat...the pitch-black cat named Mischief, who always hung around the barn, had a ring of white hairs on the very top of his head, right between the ears! And most unusual of all, Magic, who had never had the Blenheim markings, was growing a spot of white on the very top of her head, right between the ears, and had white hairs on the very tip of her feathered brown tail! We treasured these signs from Sasha, believing that she was in a happy place and sending us messages in a special and unique way.

We had always hoped that the hummingbirds would find our garden and come to drink the nectar there, but none had ever come until after Sasha died. One cool evening, a lone hummingbird came and flew around our favorite flower bush, and then flew right up into our faces. It made a sort of figure eight before it flew over and sat on the garden fence and watched us for a while, and seemed to wink at us. People told us that hummingbirds do not usually travel alone, and that they do not alight and sit on garden fences, and that they most certainly do not wink! This one did, and that is how we knew it was Sasha's spirit, in a form that could come by to visit us occasionally, to watch and wait in our garden, until we meet again.

Samantha

...a Jack Russell Terrier who lived for 16 years in Connecticut with Lorraine Moon, a registered nurse who enjoys animals, writing, and gardening.

When I was a youngster, one of our family cats returned to visit me after she died. While alive, this particular kitty had always come to my bed, purring and kneading my legs until we fell asleep together. After she died, I continued to feel her kneading and purring, and her presence was always comforting to me. My grandfather, who lived with us, also experienced an afterlife encounter with one of our cats. It may have been the same cat, but I can't remember for sure. The cat used to wait at the end of the block for my grandfather's car, and then would follow it home. Granddad drove a noisy little red car, so there was no mistaking him. Although he was not particularly fond of animals, he took great delight in espying this cat and then being greeted by her. One day while my grandfather was away, the cat suddenly became very ill and had to be euthanized. That evening my mother told Granddad that the cat had died, but he didn't believe her. He said that he had seen the cat that day, waiting for him, and that she had run to greet him as usual!

Long after my childhood, I got a very special little dog named Samantha, and I was not surprised that she, too, returned to visit me after her death. As a puppy, Samantha was so tiny I could hold her in one hand. She was an adorable, vivacious Jack Russell Terrier, and true to her breeding, she was also extremely tenacious and athletic. These aspects of her personality appeared the first night I brought her home.

I had decided my new puppy should sleep in the kitchen. I placed her bedding, water, papers, and toys on the floor, and assembled a three-foot-high gate to block the exit from the room. I had anticipated that there would be puppy howls and cries for a few nights, but that she would adjust eventually. As expected, the first night she cried, and then after a while, it was quiet. Believing all was well, and feeling quite proud that my plan was working, I turned off my lights to go to sleep. Some time later, I woke to find my new puppy jumping up and down, desperately trying to get into bed with me. "She must have knocked the gate down," I thought. "Strange that I didn't hear anything." I got up to inspect the kitchen. Everything was as it should be, including the gate, which was still affixed to the kitchen walls. I stood there perplexed, wondering how this tiny creature could have escaped. "Okay, Sam, you won this round. You can sleep with me tonight, but we're not going to make this a habit," I said. As we snuggled under the covers, I couldn't help but notice how happy she was to be in bed with me.

The next night I put her in the kitchen and checked the gate carefully to be sure that it was tightly secured against the walls. Surely no small puppy could push and squeeze through it this time. I gave the little tyke a kiss and left. As soon as I had settled into bed, I heard her running and saw her make a flying leap to land on top of my bed! "How is she getting out?" I wondered. I got out of bed to inspect the kitchen again, and found that the gate was still securely intact. Looking at the size of my pup, I decided that she was probably squeezing through the openings in the gate, even though that did not seem possible. I resolved to watch my little rascal the following night to see how she was escaping. For the second night, she happily snuggled with me and slept in my bed. It was getting to be a habit!

On the third night I put her in the kitchen, checked the gate, and turned off the light. I grabbed my flashlight and crept back to see what was going on. What I saw amazed me. My puppy was *climbing* up the side of the gate, scaling it like a rock climber! With her tiny paws she tenaciously gripped the holes, and in no time, she was up and over the barrier. Three nights! That's all it took for Samantha to assert herself as the dominant force in the family. Tough, willful, determined...that was my little Sam!

Full grown, Samantha weighed about 13 pounds. As soon as she was about a year old, I started taking her to the nursing home where I worked as a RN. Sam never liked being alone, and she always sought out the company of people and other dogs. The residents loved her because she kissed and cuddled with all of them indiscriminately. Everything went well until one day Sam collapsed unconscious at my feet. I rushed her to the vet, who suspected that she had ingested some medicine that had fallen to the floor. He hooked her up to IVs and a heart monitor and told me we'd have to "wait and see." For two days she lay unresponsive in "Puppy ICU." I remember calling the hospital late during the second night, only to have them tell me again that there was no change. I couldn't sleep and felt my hope fading with each passing hour. I cried most of the night. The next morning the phone rang. "She's awake and driving us crazy! When can you pick her up?"

Sam usually got my attention by jumping or staring at me. While she looked intently at me, I could imagine her saying, "Hey! Here I am! Look at me! Let's play and have some fun!" She was always interrupting my exercises in the morning. As I was doing my sit-ups, she stood and glared at me. If that didn't get my attention, she

pressed against me and licked my face, getting in my way completely. Once she started this, I had no choice but to stop and give her the attention she craved.

Despite her spunky, happy nature, Sam had problems with her health for most of her adult life. Even so, nothing seemed to get her down. Her seizures and allergies were controlled with medication, but when Sam was eight, the vet removed a cancerous tumor and warned me of the high probability of the cancer's returning.

Then my little dog developed arthritis and had difficulty climbing; still later, she had a liver problem because of all the medicines she had taken. The vet told me kindly that she had never seen any animal recover from such a severe liver disease. She advised me to take Samantha home, make her comfortable, and feed her an electrolyte replacement solution. There was nothing else to do but "wait and see." Once home, I mixed a rich chicken broth with electrolytes and called my creation "Samantha's Soup." Using a syringe, I force-fed her and prayed. A day later Sam was no worse, but two days later, she seemed better. After several days, she could eat and drink on her own. Months later, her liver enzymes were practically normal. Sam was an amazing dog, and her recovery defied the record books!

Sam was still taking walks with me when she was 15, but we moved at a slower pace. Sometimes I thought that the walk was too much for her, and I would pick her up. She would promptly wiggle out of my arms. She did not want any help, and would go along on her own! Unfortunately, her cancer returned, but even so, my spunky girl kept going. I dubbed her my "battery bunny dog." Some days she felt well, and other days not so well. I recall that on one of those good days, she ran and grabbed a piece of turkey out of my hand, almost taking my hand along with it!

Finally my little Samantha became very weak and could hardly move. For many weeks, I had been reluctant to euthanize her, praying that I would not have to make that decision. Now I felt I had no choice. The vet came to my house one evening, and my little dog died peacefully in my arms. Afterward I wrapped her in my sweatshirt because I wanted my arms to be around her forever. I carried her outside to be buried.

Samantha's death was an earth-shattering event for me. I felt full of pain, and my unrelenting sobs disrupted the stillness of the night. I wondered how I could live, or even take my next breath without her. Suddenly, my grief was overcome by a profound surge of joy I felt in my heart. I saw Samantha in front of me! She lingered above me, just beyond my reach. Her bright image lit up the night, and she appeared as the robust dog I had known for many years. Now free of her diseased body, she stared at me with her impish expression, as if she wanted to play. Her image stayed with me for only a minute or less, but the memory remains. She was happy and energetic once more.

About two weeks after that first vision, Samantha came to visit me again. It was early in the morning, and I was in my bedroom doing my sit-ups. I wasn't thinking about her, but suddenly I felt her close to me. Her presence was so strong it startled me. I stopped exercising and called out to her. I stretched out my hand and truly expected to feel her, but I did not. In my mind's eye, I envisioned her standing and staring at me, exactly as she used to do. Wanting to hold on to this moment, I stopped everything and sat in silence with her. For a few minutes, we shared a profound stillness and closeness. I have no doubt that she was there. Then she was gone. Afterward I felt deeply grateful that she had come to be near me again.

Samantha's final gift to me was the confirmation of existence beyond this life. Of course I felt sad for a long time, and still missed her, but knowing that we would be reunited in eternity enabled me to cope with my feelings. When I die, I expect to see Samantha at the "pearly gates." And frankly, if I don't see her, I don't want to go there!

A Horse

"The air of heaven

is that which blows between a horse's ears."

Count Bri-Dar-Kel

...an Appaloosa horse who spent most of his 17 years with Laura Uran, a RN and Animal Behavior Consultant. Laura lives in Nebraska and her hobbies include animal training, hiking, and painting. Her artwork appears in this book in several places, including the drawings of Count and Sam.

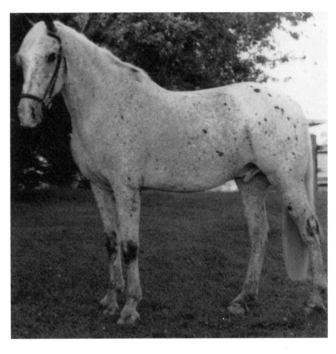

My sister and I bought Count when he was about three years old. At the time, he didn't look like much, and being an Appaloosa, he was not the breed we were looking for. We did notice, however, that he had a distinctively lush mane and tail, a beautiful head, and in spite of being too thin, he had good conformation, with strong legs and a gorgeous stride. We believed that with these traits, Count could become a good jumper as well as a dressage and pleasure horse. Just as we had expected, after medication, love, and good food, he developed into an extraordinary, elegant, athletic horse.

He was also a terrific companion, forever entertaining us with his playfulness. On pleasure rides he would often find a clod of dirt or a snowball and roll it along as he walked. He reminded us of a kid who kicks a can as he ambles along. We used to ride him in circles that spiraled in and out to enhance his flexibility and lateral bending. After a while, we began to notice that the circles often ended up larger than when we started. Suspecting that he was up to no good, we observed him carefully. Sure enough, he would occasionally take a step purposefully to increase the diameter of the circle. His shenanigans also included pretending to stub his foot at times so that he could step out a bit. He was such a clever boy!

Count was also an incorrigible prankster. One of his favorite mischievous tricks was to startle the chickens in our yard. He would begin his prank by holding water in his mouth and then intentionally rattling his almost empty food pan to attract the hens and roosters. As soon as they heard the sound, the chickens would come running and quickly gather around Count's feet, pecking at the remaining corn. Count waited patiently as more and more of them congregated around him. Then, without warning, he squirted water at them! You could almost see the grin on his face as the chickens clucked frantically, dashing in every direction.

Life was good for Count until, at age 13, he suddenly developed uveitis, an inflammatory eye disease, in one eye. Within a year, the disease had progressed to both eyes. Despite our desperate efforts to try to cure him, he was gradually losing his sight. As his vision became more limited, his lifelong pal, Shiloh, our other horse, helped him navigate the trails. Whenever my sister or I needed to take Count somewhere, he would put his nose on our shoulders trustingly, and go wherever we went. He learned quickly that "careful" meant to feel around for his footing and "step up" or "step down," meant to do just that. After four short years, our beloved horse was totally blind and in constant pain. To help him, we had two options: have his eyes removed or have him euthanized.

For most of his life Count had been able to run, play jokes, and be "King of the Pasture." Being the type of horse he was, it was difficult for him to cope with his illness and blindness. When it became apparent that he had no quality of life, my sister and I felt it would be best to euthanize him. I didn't stay around for the procedure. I just couldn't bear to see this once robust animal and friend fall to the ground. As a tribute to him, my family held a brief ceremony and put his name on a memorial brick at our Humane Society.

About two weeks after Count's death, I was riding Shiloh into one of our favorite fields. The day was bright, clear, and dry, with no hint of fog or moisture. Moving through the area where Count always liked to gallop, I saw a mist appear suddenly, about ten feet to the right of me. It floated along with Shiloh and me, and then moved ahead. I couldn't help but notice that the colors in the haze reminded me of Count — white with hints of brown patches. My horse began to whinny, letting me know that he wanted to gallop and catch up with the cloud. I let him go. We caught up, and for a few minutes we moved together, until I noticed the mist begin to fade, and then it abruptly disappeared. Once it was gone, Shiloh slowed down and whinnied repeatedly, looking all around. Eventually he stopped, sighed deeply, and lowered his head with his ears drooping. I dismounted. The two of us just stood there for some time. I believe the mist was Count. Shiloh's reaction proved that to me. I remember thinking, "So good to fly through the fields with you one last time, Count!"

The next day before I turned Shiloh out, his head shot up and he neighed and pranced excitedly. I looked to the distance, where Shiloh was looking. There, on the top of a hill, I saw a fuzzy image. It appeared to be a brown and white horse, galloping. Shiloh and I watched the image quietly until it faded. I believe this was another visitation from Count. Shiloh and I were fortunate to see our friend again, this time galloping in his free-flowing manner, back home to God.

Later, as I thought about these events, I felt honored and humbled. I wondered why Count had returned to visit us. Perhaps he came to show us that he was well, happy, and grateful to be free of his pain. Seeing him so robust again gave my heart a lift and allowed me to feel better about our decision to have him euthanized. Perhaps he returned to cheer his faithful companion, Shiloh. Or perhaps Count, who always loved a good joke, figured that surprising us in this manner would be his final prank!

Cats

"Of all God's creatures, there is only one that cannot

be made the slave of the leash. That one is the cat.

If man could be crossed with the cat, it would improve man,

but deteriorate the cat."

Mark Twain

Stormy

...a silver lining in the clouds of life, Stormy was a green-eyed cat who owned my mother for 12 years, and who did not leave our family even after his death. Erin Wade, a secretary who is part of that Texas family, tells her story.

Stormy was a beautiful, silvery gray cat with long, wispy hair and bluish green eyes. He arrived at my mother's doorstep unexpectedly one year around Thanksgiving. When Mother answered the doorbell, she found a little girl, about seven or eight years old, holding a tiny gray kitten. Mother had never seen the girl anywhere in the neighborhood. The girl looked up at my mother and asked, "Is this your kitty? I just found him close to your house."

"No," my mother replied. "He doesn't belong to me."

The little girl had tears in her eyes, and confided that she couldn't keep the kitten. "Would you please take care of him until I find the owner?" she asked. "I'm afraid to leave him alone because he might get hurt."

Mother took the kitten, and the child never returned. The little gray fur-ball remained with my mother as a wonderful companion for many years.

I moved my family — two boys and a cat — back to live with my mother after enduring 13 years of a bad marriage. As soon as I entered the house, Stormy made it clear to my cat that he was the boss. My mother's cat already knew that. Stormy was petite, but his "big hair" and the way he carried himself made everyone think he was huge, and Stormy certainly believed that!

I grew fond of Stormy quickly, and he seemed to like me, too, because he frequently slept with me. I always knew he was coming when his claws hit my wooden bed frame and made a distinct "clicking" sound. Every time I heard that click, I would smile, knowing that Stormy would soon be cuddling close to me.

About two years after I moved in with my mom, Stormy's health began to fail. He stopped eating and had trouble urinating. When Mom took him to the vet, she learned that he had kidney failure. The vet had several ideas for treatment, so my mother decided to leave Stormy with her, and we prayed for a miracle. When Mom visited him the next day, however, he was so sick he didn't even try to lick the food she placed on his nose. None of the medicines seemed to be helping, and he appeared to be suffering. This broke my mother's heart, and she decided it was time to let him go. While the vet gave him the injection, she held Stormy facing my mother so they would be able to see each other as he went to sleep.

The experience was extremely hard on my mother, but at least she was with him at the end. When I came home from work and learned that Stormy was gone, I was very upset about not being there for him and my mom. That evening, my mom and I had a really good cry together. Our home was filled with sadness, as if a black cloud were hanging over everything.

A few nights after Stormy's death, I lay in bed trying to go to sleep. Suddenly I heard a familiar "clicking" sound on my bed frame. "Oh, here comes Stormy," I thought. I felt him on the bed as he walked around in a circle and settled down on the side of my leg, just as he had done many times before. Then I remembered that Stormy was dead, and I suddenly felt petrified! I didn't move a muscle, and could hardly breathe as I continued to feel his weight against my leg. I knew it couldn't be any of the other cats because they were with my mother. I finally turned quickly and flipped the light on. I saw nothing. "Just my imagination," I mumbled and went to sleep.

Imagination? I would still believe that if it weren't for a second experience. Two nights later, it happened again. This time I didn't hear the claws clicking on the bed frame, but I suddenly sensed Stormy's presence and then became aware of his weight as he cuddled against me, just as he used to do. Lying quite still, I began to feel a soft, rumbling vibration on my skin. Stormy was purring! Slowly I reached down to where I thought he was. I felt something — not fur or even a solid form, but something I can only describe as a ball of energy. The sensation reminded me of the feeling you get when you try to push two opposing magnets together. A chill rushed over me. There was no question in my mind. It was Stormy! Then, all the sensations stopped, and Stormy was gone.

Relaxing against the pillow, I felt comforted by the visitation because I knew that Stormy had come to say goodbye and that he was all right. One of the greatest compliments a human being can receive is the unconditional love of an animal. Stormy gave me this gift. I was now able to say "farewell" to him, believing that our paths would cross again in another world.

Pushy and *Purrl*

...two tabby cats whose human, Marie Ehrenberg, is a retired employee of the Mayo Clinic in Minnesota. Pushy lived to be 13, and Purrl was still alive at the time this story was written.

Many years ago, I heard a kitten crying somewhere across the street from my house. When I went to investigate, I discovered an adorable little orange tabby that apparently had been abandoned. Something seemed to click between us, causing me to bond with her immediately even though I had never owned a kitty. I decided to keep this orange bundle of joy as an outdoor cat. She earned her name soon after she came into my yard. With her tail held high, and with all the superiority a cat can display, she simply took over, as if she were the new owner of the place and all residents were firmly under her paw. Even the dogs — one of them a German Shepherd — accepted her dominance immediately! I named my new friend "Pushy Cat"!

I built an area for her in my garage, affectionately named "Pushy's Hut." It consisted of a dog kennel lined with insulation material and towels on the kennel floor for her bed. I set out two bowls, one for food and the other for water. Pushy Cat lived happily this way for 13 years. She always stayed close to my yard and home, and I saw her daily. She would come into the yard to sit in my lap or just stick around to see was what I was doing in the garden. She became a part of my routine, and I always looked forward to seeing her.

Then one year just before Christmas, she suddenly disappeared. I had last seen her about ten o'clock in the morning, and then she was gone. I searched everywhere for her, to no avail. She was not in the field across the street, and she would not have strayed farther than my yard. Perhaps someone had picked her up and taken her to a home too far from my house for her to find her way back, I thought. I hoped that she hadn't been hurt, and that she might  even have been a Christmas gift for a little child. I truly mourned the loss of this cat, and always wondered what had happened to her.

About four years after Pushy's disappearance, I took a workshop in animal communication. It was an intensive two-day course involving a lot of meditation. In the last exercise, we were supposed to try to connect with a specific animal. Immediately I thought of Pushy Cat. As soon as I settled into my meditation, she suddenly appeared. I watched as she sashayed up to the gate of my house, coming right toward me. All the while, she held her tail straight up in the air and curved to the right, just as she had done so many years before. She looked very healthy as she continued to trot toward me. But once she was within a few inches of me, she abruptly disappeared and seemed to dissolve into a kind of gray cloud. The entire episode was so short and simple, and yet so powerful. I knew that what I had experienced was not a dream or a vision or just thinking of her. It seemed as if I had left my own reality and entered hers. I believe the meditation allowed me to visit Pushy Cat on her plane, which differed from that of the living. I have no doubt she was actually there!

What joy I felt, seeing that Pushy Cat was all right! Her message was clear: "Hey, Marie. Look at me. I'm fine. Now don't mourn for me any longer." After this experience, I felt emotionally ready to get another cat. The following week I went to the pound, and although I looked at every cat, I felt no sense of connection with any of them. Nothing clicked as it had before with Pushy. When I went back to the pound again, it was the day before Thanksgiving. Now there were many more cats available, and one of them was a little orange tabby whose color reminded me of Pushy. I had decided she would be my new feline companion, but while I was holding her, I felt a strong compulsion to turn around and look at the little gray kitten I had seen before. To my surprise, she was on her side, looking at me and rubbing against the floor of the cage, begging me to choose her. As soon as I saw her behaving like that, I changed my mind. I knew she was the one for me.

On the way home, I suddenly recalled that when I had seen Pushy Cat in my meditative state, she had evaporated into a sort of gray cloud! Now I understood the meaning of that gray cloud. I felt sure that Pushy had instructed me to choose this gray tabby. The certainty of my conviction was strengthened further when I got home. As soon as I set the carrier down in the garage and let my new kitten out, she ran directly to Pushy's Hut!

As I sat with my new companion the night before Thanksgiving, and felt her warmth and heard her purring in

my lap, I reflected on what had happened to me. I recalled that special visit from Pushy and what a blessing it was to receive her two messages: "Don't mourn anymore because I'm okay," and "Your new cat will be gray." And then I smiled as the thought came to me, that Pushy Cat was on the Other Side, still giving me orders!

I've named my new cat "Purrl." Certainly, at this point, the question of reincarnation stirs in my mind. I do not know if I believe in reincarnation, but if it exists, then I think there is a strong possibility that Purrl is the reincarnation of Pushy. In any case, I don't believe in coincidence. I know I was meant to have this little gray cat, and I am so pleased to have found her.

Chaucer

...a red tabby cat who lived in Texas with his guardian, Marsha J. West, a beloved feline friend, Seraphina, and Cairn Terriers named Margaret and Speeder. Marsha's interests are numerous and she is a great lover of animals.

Chaucer was a beautiful red tabby cat. My favorite thing to say to him was, "Who would make a red cat with a pink nose and yellow eyes? But hey, on you it works!" In response, Chaucer would purr. Despite a short life of only five years, Chaucer made a deep impact on all the members of our family. Everyone adored him, especially my sister, Ladis. Chaucer and my sister had such a strong bond, they were like one soul. Once when Ladis was hospitalized for six days, Chaucer moped around and refused to eat, drink, or move from my sister's bed. For days he just lay on her t-shirt, waiting for her to come home. Once she returned, his world was complete again.

Our cat, Seraphina, also had a special bond with Chaucer. Seraphina was our little sprite, forever running, playing, and acting silly and joyful. Almost every evening, she and Chaucer played together, often with their little squeaky toy, Mousie. They would race up and down the stairs or go into their favorite place, the dining room, where jumping on the table and chairs made their games even more fun. When they

finished playing, Chaucer would lead the way to the litter box in the laundry room. Seraphina was afraid of the laundry room, but with her companion protecting her, she was brave enough to go in.

Chaucer was quite adept at getting into the pantry where we stored the snacks for our dogs and cats. Whenever he wanted a snack, he would lie on his back, slip his right paw under the louvered door, pull the door open, and then jump up onto the pantry shelf. Once there, he would toss the package of treats to the floor so that our dogs could open it. Afterward, both cats and dogs consumed the tasty morsels that scattered on the floor. Chaucer especially liked "Boo Baas," a dried lamb treat, which we kept in a Tupperware container; otherwise he would get into them all the time.

One night, just past midnight, Ladis awoke to hear a dragging and thumping noise. Next she heard a loud "clunk." Wondering what in the heck was going on, she turned on the light. There in the middle of her room sat Chaucer, looking at her with the Tupperware container next to him! Ladis figured that the little rascal had pushed the Boo Baas onto the floor and then, holding the plastic box with his little teeth, he had dragged it a very long way from the kitchen to her bedroom. Having reached his destination with the prize, he had *somehow* flung the container over the four-foot child's gate that was across the entrance to her room. Now, sitting before her in the middle of the night, Chaucer was pleading with her to open the Tupperware and give him some Boo Baas! Ladis laughed and laughed and, of course, rewarded his efforts with a handful of the savory treats. Then she hugged him and told him what a smart cat he was. Indeed, both Ladis and I knew that Chaucer had to be an "old soul," because he was so confident and intelligent.

Although my vet kept insisting that Chaucer was healthy, I had a hunch that something was wrong. We took him to several vets, but none of them confirmed my suspicion. Even after Chaucer's stomach bloated, the doctor was unsure of the cause, and sent him home without any specific treatment. By the next morning, he was wheezing and gasping for air. We rushed him to another vet, who suspected that a spider might have bitten him. The vet assured us that he would recover with treatment, so we left him at the hospital. We had no sooner returned home than we received a horrible phone call. Chaucer was dying! Stunned by the horrible message, we rushed back to be with him during his last moments.

As we gathered around him, I noticed how beautiful he looked, with his red hair shimmering and glowing. Ladis and I told him we loved him, and would see him again, and urged him to go to the Light. Chaucer looked at me and then at my sister. Then he turned his head to the left and gazed upward, his yellow eyes growing bigger and brighter, as if he saw something wonderful and familiar. His eyes seemed to show a glimmer of recognition. I believe at that point someone came to meet him. Suddenly, his eyes glazed over, and he was gone.

Chaucer's death was a sudden and overwhelming shock for the whole family, but the one who seemed most affected was little Seraphina. Once Chaucer was gone, she changed abruptly and only wanted to stay, isolated, in the dining room. She would not use the litter box in the laundry room unless Ladis or I went with her. The vet said he had never seen such grief in an animal. He also commented that although animals have a strong instinct for survival, he thought Seraphina actually wanted to die. It broke our hearts to see her mourn like that.

Not long after Chaucer died, I began to sense his presence in our house. It occurred to me that maybe this was why Seraphina was spending so much time in the dining room. I decided to sneak in there to check out my suspicion. One evening, I entered the dining room quietly. The room was dimly lit, but I could see Seraphina, who was sitting on a chair at the head of the table, gazing upward. Then I saw Chaucer! He was on top of the table, close to her. The two cats were face to face, and there was obviously some communication going on between them. As I came closer, Chaucer turned his head to glance at me, but he quickly looked away to continue focusing his attention on Seraphina. I moved closer, and was about eight feet from Chaucer, who appeared as a solid, three-dimensional figure. I could even see the texture of his coat. I took a few more steps, stopped, and spoke softly to him. "Chaucer, you must leave now, and Seraphina cannot go with you." I hated to tell him to leave, but he no longer belonged with us. As soon as I uttered these words, his image disappeared.

I never saw Chaucer again, but Seraphina continued to stay by herself in the dining room, so I was sure Chaucer was still coming to her. To make matters worse, her health was beginning to deteriorate. In a desperate effort to help her, I decided to give Chaucer another strong message to leave, even though it was painful for me.

I entered the dining room and immediately felt Chaucer's presence, so I began to talk to him. I told him I loved him, but I said, "Chaucer, you are dead and you don't belong here. You must leave and go to Heaven. We love you, but by staying here, you are making Seraphina sick. It is not her time to go. I wish you could stay, but you can't. You must go now. We will see each other again." As I left the dining room, I took Seraphina with me, and after that, whenever she isolated herself in the dining room, either Ladis or I would remove her and bring her back to be with us.

My sister also experienced an afterlife contact with Chaucer. She told me at first that it was a dream, but later confessed she was sure that it really happened. She awoke to find Chaucer beside her. Her face was buried in his neck so that she could smell him. She could feel the warmth of his body and his soft hair as he lay next to her. She recalls that he was purring and that he pushed his face into and under her hand, just as he had done when he was alive. Ladis cupped her fingers around his face and rubbed him. She remembers breathing his air and kissing him. Then he was gone. Afterward my sister sobbed because she missed him so much.

Seraphina is finally doing better now that three years have passed. Although she occasionally acts like a little sprite again, she will never be the same as when Chaucer was alive. A part of her died when he left. She still fears the laundry room and sneaks off to spend time alone in the dining room, as if she is still waiting for her friend to come back.

Barnaby

...a cat with a remarkable personality, who lived for 15 years in Pennsylvania with Susan Goodman, a special education teacher, and her husband, David.

My husband and I got our first cat, Barnaby, soon after we were married. Our boy Barnaby was a big, friendly cat with a voracious appetite, and he was never particular about what he ate. One evening after making lasagna, I foolishly placed it on the kitchen table while I tossed the salad. Before the family had a chance to sit down to eat, Barnaby had jumped up and was standing in the casserole dish, licking his chops. "What are you doing? Get out of there," I yelled, shooing him away. Barnaby sprang from the middle of the lasagna and ran around the house, flinging cheese and tomato sauce everywhere! Barnaby also liked the taste of tobacco! If a friend brought a purse into our house, Barnaby would slink toward the bag and quickly plunge his face into the various compartments of the bag. He went through all manner of gymnastics in the desperate hope of finding his favorite thing to eat — cigarettes! Oh, how he loved them! Given the chance, he would have eaten each one right down to its corky filter. The tobacco seems to have been tamed by stomach juices peculiar to Barnaby, as he never got sick.

Barnaby always kept us chuckling with his unusual personality. Without a doubt, his most hilarious and endearing antic was playing the batter in our make-believe baseball game. We began the game by putting a small red cap, decorated with a large letter "P" for Philadelphia Phillies, on Barnaby's head. With his hat securely in place, the cat took his position on our kitchen countertop. Then my husband and I would toss ice chips at him, while Barnaby took swings at the chips with his two front paws. He really looked as if he were batting the tiny pieces of ice and, in fact, became quite good at hitting "home runs"! We recorded the scenario on videotape so that we could continue to have many good laughs in the future.

When Barnaby was ten, one day my mother-in-law commented that he appeared to be losing weight, which was quite a feat for a cat who ate so much and so indiscriminately. Indeed, we discovered that he did have a medical problem, hyperthyroidism. The vet put him on medication, which kept him well for about four years until other health problems began to develop. His kidneys began to fail, and his back legs became so limp he couldn't jump. About the same time, our female cat, Brandi, had been diagnosed with cancer. We had thought Brandi would go first because of her illness, but we were wrong. Soon the vet told us that Barnaby had only a few days to live, so we decided to have him euthanized. I had never experienced this before, and wanted to hold him as it was done. I remember that it was New Year's Eve, but there was no celebrating for us. Not long afterward, Brandi also passed away. We buried the two cats side by side in a pet cemetery and had a marker put in place inscribed:

Barnaby   Brandi
Friends and Companions
Loved by Susan and David Goodman

We did not talk about "replacing" our cats, our first "babies," so consequently, there were no animals in the house for some time. About four months after we lost Brandi, I was getting ready to go to the school where I worked as a special education teacher. My first class was later in the morning, and my husband had already left for work. For some reason, I suddenly had an overwhelming urge to play the videotape of Barnaby wearing his red baseball cap and batting at the ice chips. As I was watching it, I became aware of a noise in the hallway right next to the bedroom. I stopped the video and listened. Again I heard the sound — pitter-patter, pitter-patter, as if an animal was walking with light footsteps. Then I heard a tinkling noise that sounded like Barnaby was close by. Whenever Barnaby used to walk, the tag on his collar would hit the buckle, making that exact sound.

I felt eerie. "What's going on? Are you there, Barnaby?" I wondered. Despite feeling a bit "spooked," I went to search for a cat that couldn't possibly be there. As I walked down the hallway, I continued to hear the footsteps and the tinkling of the tag. I somehow sensed that Barnaby was near, but I couldn't see him anywhere. The sounds lasted about a minute, and then silence filled my home. Looking out the window, I noticed it was snowing — unusual for that time of year. I finished dressing and left for work.

Once I got to school, I temporarily forgot my morning's experience, but immediately after work, the whole episode played again in my mind. I rushed to my husband's place of business to tell him what had happened. Several people in the office listened and a lively discussion followed, with everyone questioning me and making comments. One person asked me if this day was special in any way. I thought for a moment, and then it hit me. It certainly was a special day. "It's April eighteenth, Barnaby's birthday!" I exclaimed, as chills ran throughout my body. Barnaby had come back on his birthday to let me know that he was still around!

" A very slight veil separates us from the 'loved and lost.'"

...Mary Todd Lincoln

Puff

...a special white cat who lived with Bonnie Trowbridge for 16 years. Bonnie, who is a grants administrator and medical secretary, treasured every hour with this enchanting creature.

Puff came into my life when I was married to an abusive man and pregnant with my second child. My cruel husband delighted in upsetting me to make my asthma worse. He would take my inhaler away and taunt me, saying, "You can't breathe now, can you?" or "You're going to die!" Then one day, a tiny white kitten about five weeks old appeared in my front yard. As no one else claimed him, I made him a part of our family and named him "Puff." He grew to be a comfort to me during this horrible time, and was wonderfully gentle with my children. Since he had literally appeared out of nowhere, I believe he was a gift from God to help me cope with my difficult situation. By the time I finally got the courage to divorce my husband, Puff was nine years old.

The next six years were blissfully happy, living with Puff and my children. Eventually I remarried and added a wonderful new husband to my life. But everything changed when Puff's health began to decline. It was hard for me to accept his condition, and the thought of losing him was more than I could bear. I had depended on him for so long that somehow I had convinced myself that he would live forever. I took Puff to a vet, who could find nothing seriously wrong. Later when Puff stopped eating and could barely drag himself around, I rushed him to another vet, who decided to keep him in order to perform several tests. Shortly after I left, the vet called to tell me that Puff was dying! Shocked and hysterical, I hurried to the clinic, but it was too late. Puff was gone.

The circumstances of his death broke my heart. Puff had been my feline soul mate for 16 years. Many times when my husband was abusing me both mentally and physically, Puff had been my only lifeline. Now I felt that I had betrayed him by not being with him when he died. I felt so guilty, and wondered if he could ever forgive me.

About two years after Puff died, I became quite ill. Everyone thought I had the flu, but I didn't get better. Finally, my situation worsened and I had to be rushed to the hospital, where I was diagnosed with spinal meningitis. It was uncertain whether or not I would survive. I lay in a coma, close to death, and although I was completely unaware of my physical surroundings, I clearly remember a bright light whose glow was magnificent, unlike anything I had ever seen. I could look directly at it, but it did not hurt my eyes. Enticed and enchanted by the light, I began to walk toward it. Then in the distance in front of me, I saw Puff! "Oh, my God, Puff is here!" I said. I was overjoyed and my only desire was to get to him. As I hurried forward, he walked across my path. His silhouette was clear, and I distinctly remember how high he carried his tail. "Nothing is going to keep me from him," I thought. But then Puff turned and walked away from me. I stopped. Somehow I understood that he was telling me to turn around. Just as he instructed, I walked back through what seemed to be a tunnel, away from the light, and away from Puff. I believe that Puff saved my life! The doctor told me later that this was the turning point in my illness, when I began to get better.

As a result of my encounter, I have become a more caring and loving person. My life is happy with my second husband, and I devote much of my time to taking care of our animals. Before this near-death experience, I wasn't sure there was an afterlife for pets, but now I am *certain* one exists. When I pass away, I know that Puff will be there to greet me again. What a joyous reunion that will be! For now, he is waiting on the Other Side until we are together again. I have no doubt that other people will also be greeted by their pets, as they cross over into eternity.

Puff is buried in a box that my husband made especially for him. I put one of my favorite bracelets inside the box as my way of keeping a part of me always with my special friend. We have a lovely site in our garden, dedicated to the memory of this beloved cat. There is a raised bed of flowers, a gazing globe, and a statue of an angel with a wooden cat next to it — white, of course, like Puff.

Corky

...an Abyssinian cat who lived for almost ten years with Karen Bunkowski in Florida. Karen is an artist who paints mostly in watercolor, with animals being her favorite subjects.

One look at that beautiful Abyssinian face and I was hooked! I first saw these cats at a breed show and immediately fell in love. Later, I purchased my first Abyssinian cat from a local breeder, who chose one of the kittens for me. He was not show quality, but I could not have been happier with my new, ruddy companion whom I named Corky. He was three months old — affectionate, playful, inquisitive, and gorgeous!

I remember the first time my new kitty saw snowflakes. He jumped into the air and tried to catch them. As soon as he thought he had one, it would disappear and he would look all around for it. Once he realized he hadn't caught anything, he'd jump at another snowflake, only to repeat the same experience. He just wouldn't stop, and I couldn't stop laughing!

Corky was a determined hunter who loved to chase all small, moving things, especially birds. One cold winter day, I couldn't find him until I discovered him perched on top of my birdfeeder, just beyond my reach. It took me several hours of coaxing with a tasty morsel to finally get him to come down. By that time, he was so cold he had frostbite on the tips of his long ears! Another time Corky had jumped into my swimming pool, hoping to catch some frogs. It was a warm, summer evening, and their croaking could be heard all over the neighborhood. Although he tried very hard to capture them, the frogs were too quick and too slippery. He gave the game up and emerged from the pool, dripping wet and very unhappy!

In no time, I grew to feel closer to Corky than any other living creature, and I honestly believe he felt the same way about me. When Corky was three, I purchased another Abyssinian cat, Dandy. Just as I had hoped, the cats quickly became buddies. One of their favorite places to play was a beach close to my house. They would run and chase each other along the sand until they were almost too tired to move. After a brief rest, the feline pals would wade into the bay to hunt for fish. It always brought me joy to see them cavorting together!

Despite his prowess as a hunter, Corky had a loving disposition and an endearing habit that earned him the nickname "Velcro Cat." Whenever I moved around the house, cleaning, vacuuming, doing the laundry or other chores, Corky would wrap his front legs around my neck and press his little belly tightly against my chest. As he was holding on, he would rub his head against me. If anyone pulled him off, Corky would cling to that person in exactly the same way. It didn't matter whom he was stuck to, Corky was truly one serious Velcro Cat!

Corky slept with me, and regularly woke me every morning at four o'clock to feed him. As soon as he was ready to eat, he would stroll across the bed toward me in the hopes of waking me up. Sometimes his walking woke me, but if that did not work, he would stand on my chest. If I still did not respond (or was pretending to be asleep), he would touch my head with his paw. When, after several pats on my head, growing increasingly harder, I still did not react, he would bite me! It was never really a hard bite, just a little nibble.

Abyssinians are prone to liver disease, and unfortunately, Corky was plagued with this problem. He had been on one medication or another throughout most of his life. When I realized that it was hurting him to jump, and saw his skin turning yellow, I knew that Corky would never get better, and that he should be euthanized. I chose to have him experience this inevitable transition at home, and I made sure that Corky's running and fishing companion, Dandy, had a chance to see the body. My grief was almost unbearable. Then, just a year later, I lost Dandy, too.

About two years after Corky passed away, I began to be aware of a recurring dream about him, but I suspect that less intense versions of the same dream had occurred earlier. As time went on, the dream became more vivid, occurring every few weeks over a period of four years. At first, the dream was a nightmare. It would begin with Corky jumping on my bed and walking toward me. Suddenly I would imagine that Dandy and my other deceased cats were still alive, but that I had forgotten to feed them. I would be rushing around trying to find food for them just before I woke up. A terrible guilty feeling burdened me until I realized it was just a dream.

Eventually, the dream no longer included the part about not feeding the other cats, but Corky's jumping on the bed and walking toward me remained. It became more intense with each successive dream, so much so that I actually began to feel each step Corky took, and I would wake up fully expecting to see him. The dream was short but powerful. I just *knew* Corky was there, and I was always disappointed to wake up and not see him. One day I was determined to wake up in time to see and talk to him before he left. The next morning as expected, here came Corky. As he jumped onto the bed, I felt it shake, and I even heard the sheets move with each step he took toward me. Just as I had planned, I forced myself to wake up and sat bolt upright, expecting to see Corky or at least the indentations in the sheets. Even though I did not see him or the marks of his feet on the sheets, I *felt* his presence. I felt so blessed to have this visitation that I quickly thanked him over and over again.

After that, I *never* had the dream again. I had dreamt it every few weeks for four years, and suddenly it was gone! I believe that when I spoke to Corky and acknowledged his visitation, he knew that I had finally received his message. He had come to soothe my grief and let me know that he still existed. Once I acknowledged him, he said his goodbye for now and "I love you." Sometimes I am sorry that I spoke, if that is what caused the dreams to stop. I loved dreaming about him because it comforted me and made me feel as if we were together again. But I understand that there is no need for Corky to keep coming back. He knows that I finally got the message. Corky has moved on to "dance the spiral," in the beautiful place where, I believe, all living things go after they die. Corky and I are still bound by the deep love we shared for one another, and I believe we will be together again some day.

Flower and *Shelby*

...two special cats owned by Ellen Bogner, a RN who teaches medical terminology at a local college in Wisconsin. The National Wildlife Federation has certified Ellen and her husband's backyard as a "wildlife habitat."

For 21 years, I had a tiny calico cat named Flower. She weighed no more than six pounds, but despite her small size, she possessed a lot of attitude, or as I called it, "catitude." The two of us lived happily in one home for 13 years until I got married and moved into my husband's house. Flower was most unhappy about the move, but even more upsetting to her was the presence of my husband's large Yellow Lab, Boo. To let us know of her displeasure, Flower protested mightily by staying under our bed and never moving from this spot, even to eat. I had to place her food and litter box next to her, and I was worried that she might not survive.

But after a month in isolation, Flower surprised us by suddenly coming out of her room. We watched as she walked boldly up to Boo, whacked her across the nose, and meowed something that I'm sure is not printable! In that singular moment, Flower proclaimed her position as primary animal in our new household. She taught us a lesson. It's okay to spend time hiding and regrouping, but some day you have to come out fighting to claim your place. My Flower was back, oozing with "catitude"!

Following that ordeal, Flower enjoyed many peaceful and happy years in her new home. Although she was a small creature, she loved to eat, with breakfast being her favorite meal. But one evening she unexpectedly vomited her dinner and then stayed under our bed instead of sleeping with us. Even though she greeted me the next morning and was quite responsive, I knew she was not feeling well because she did not want to eat breakfast. Before I went to work, I checked to see how she was doing. She had crawled back under the bed and was asleep. I left, thinking she would surely be better by the time I returned home.

My day at work went along as usual until late in the afternoon when I suddenly felt extremely tired and drained of energy. I thought I was going to faint. As my feeling of exhaustion continued, I became frightened and thought, "If this continues, I'll have to go to the emergency room." But then, slowly, my strength began to return.

As I began to feel better, I suddenly saw an image of Flower in my mind. She was under the bed and lying on her side. I knew something was wrong. Moments later I left work and rushed home. There was Flower, under the bed and on her side, exactly as I had seen her in my vision! She was barely alive, and passed away a few minutes later.

In the moment when I felt exhausted, I believe Flower had a heart attack or stroke. Remarkable as it seems, I had felt the waning of her life in my own body! Somehow, she communicated with me, calling me home to be with her in the last moments. We had lived together for more than 21 years, and she had been healthy and active up to her last two days. I was grateful that she had died this way and thankful for having and loving her for such a long time. We buried Flower in our backyard, and engraved on her tombstone is the advice to "Take Time to Smell the Flowers."

When Flower was about 18, another cat joined our household. He appeared unexpectedly in our yard on an extremely hot summer afternoon, and had obviously been on his own for a long time. He was pitifully thin and covered with sores. We named him Shelby. After being treated with antibiotics and love, he recovered and turned out to be an absolutely gorgeous fluff-ball, a longhaired cat with a leonine presence. I later discovered that he was a Norwegian Forest cat, an expensive and uncommon breed in the United States. Not only was he a beautiful cat, he was also sweet and gentle. We referred to him affectionately as our "Saint Francis Cat" because he never showed any aggression toward other creatures. Birds and squirrels could venture close to him, and he never chased them away. We also called him "The Shelbs" because, like "The Donald," he had a commanding presence, and the most unusual things happened around him!

There are many trees in our backyard, which helps to create a safe haven for animals, and for years I have put bread and cat food on my patio to attract the various creatures to the neighborhood. In the evening, I like to sit on a recliner next to the window and watch the drama unfold in the lighted area of the patio. Normally, the critters, especially the raccoons, squabble over the food, but one night it was different. A stray cat and three raccoons were eating together peacefully, and Shelby was sitting quietly on the side of the patio, watching the animals huddle together as they ate. His presence seemed to calm the visitors as they shared the food. Suddenly a skunk appeared and approached the group. "Uh-Oh," I thought. "Surely all the animals including Shelby will scamper away now." But that did not happen. None of the animals moved, except for one raccoon who scooted a little to the side to allow the skunk to join in and eat the bread! Shelby continued to sit quietly, as if presiding over his court. I was deeply touched as I watched this tranquil assembly. I felt as if I had been given a glimpse of Heaven, where "the wolf also shall dwell with the lamb, and the leopard shall lie down with the kid." I believe that what I saw was possible because Shelby was there.

Some years later, in the month of April, Shelby stopped eating, and his health worsened rapidly. The vet prescribed medication so I could take care of him at home. He lasted only a few days before slipping into a coma and then dying. We buried him in our backyard close to Flower and our statue of St. Francis, an appropriate resting place for our "Saint Francis Cat."

His death occurred at an incredibly difficult time for me. Not only did Shelby die, but my grandmother also died, and four teenagers from our small community were killed in a car accident. Overwhelmed by so much tragedy, I didn't take time to grieve properly over Shelby's death.

A year later, close to the anniversary of Shelby's death, I felt renewed grief, as if he had just died. I went to bed missing him and feeling depressed. Some time in the early morning I awoke. I was lying on my right side as usual, and to my surprise, I felt Shelby lying next to me, close to the crook of my arm! I am sure it was he, because I recognized his snoring and loud purring. I began to pet him and remember feeling the unusual texture of his fur — the long, coarse hairs on top with shorter, softer hairs underneath. As I was touching him, I felt the warmth of his large body. For a few minutes I stroked him, comforted by his presence. Then I had to prove to myself that it was really Shelby and not my other cat, Sweet Clover, who typically slept in that spot. I moved my hand farther down my body, and there, I felt Sweet Clover. She was lying next to Shelby, and I knew it was she because her coat was soft and fluffy all over, with no long, coarse outer hairs. Feeling peaceful and contented, I fell asleep again.

I believe the death of a beloved animal is the hardest death to endure. Unlike your children and human friends, pets remain close, loving, and dependent upon you for their entire life, growing ever dearer as they age. I have never told anyone about this experience before now! I didn't want this precious encounter with Shelby to be discounted or ridiculed in any way. Somehow, Shelby knew I was grieving, and he came to comfort me. Believe me when I say that Shelby was there! I have no doubt. I also have no doubt that he continues to exist in some form in the Kingdom on the Other Side.

> "The grave itself is but a covered bridge, leading from light to light, through a brief darkness."
>
> …Henry Wadsworth Longfellow

Bone

...a Flamepoint Ragdoll-mix cat, owned for almost 17 years by Melissa Zobell, who works in animal rescue.

One day, to my surprise, I found a tiny, peach-colored kitten under a rosebush in my yard. I have no clue how he got there, but he came at the right time, just when I desperately needed him. I was 15 and having a hard time growing up, even to the point of my feeling suicidal at times. Without telling anyone, I sneaked the little kitten into the house. Having this creature to love and care for changed my life, and gave me a reason to live. A powerful closeness developed between us, so much so that I often felt as if he was an extension of my own body.

Bone, as I came to call him, grew up to be a beautiful Flamepoint Ragdoll-mix cat with splendid peach coloring. He was so gorgeous that I often referred to him as "my handsome man." He was also very affectionate and when he wanted attention, it was almost impossible to push him away. His most unusual trait was a distinct "mrr-mrr" sound. Before uttering this sound, he always pursed his mouth and moved his whiskers forward. I have rescued hundreds of cats, but I have seen that familiar facial grimace and heard that distinct "mrr-mrr" sound come only from one other cat.

We had many good years together, but as Bone grew older, he developed diabetes.

By the time he was 16, his world had narrowed to my bedroom, where his food and water and litter box were placed beside my bed. Even though he was very ill, I had hoped to have him another year. Unfortunately, that hope vanished the day my husband, children, and I moved into our new house. Our moving day was chaotic to say the least. The flooding of the basement in our old home only added to the confusion. Everyone was stressed, including the animals, who could sense a change was coming. When I had to run some last-minute errands, I left Bone in my bedroom and put my dogs into another bedroom behind a closed door. Bone was accustomed to living with dogs because I had been involved with animal rescue for many years and often had visiting canines, as well as our own. He got along well with them, but I would never have left him in the same room. When I returned home, I saw, to my horror, that the doors had not been firmly closed, and the dogs had escaped from their room and had killed Bone!

What had happened to my precious, handsome boy was unthinkable! He had been there for me over many years, and now I had let him down. Feelings of guilt and remorse swept over me as I thought of how I could have prevented this accident. If only I had been more careful. If only I had checked the doors once more before I left. Along with my guilt came a great deal of anger toward the dogs. I believe the stress of the move contributed to the attack, and of course, Bone was an obvious target because he was so old and weak. My husband and I took Bone's body with us when we moved so that we could bury him in our new backyard.

Four days later, and now in my new home, I was sitting beside the bathtub watching my youngest child play in his bath. The bathroom was situated in the middle of a hallway, and the door was open that morning.

Suddenly, from the corner of my eye, I saw Bone! I glanced up to see him take a few long strides and stop in front of the bathroom door, holding his back leg out in his typical pose. The vision of Bone in the doorway was distinct. We actually made eye contact and then he disappeared. Everything I witnessed was characteristic of his behavior when he was alive — walking with a long stride, stopping frequently to extend one of his hind legs, and then looking around before he continued on his way. Nothing was unusual about what I saw, except that Bone was dead!

There were no more apparitions until about a year later, when my husband, Kurtis, saw Bone. It was close to midnight, and all our cats had settled down from their nightly escapades. Kurtis walked out of the kitchen and glanced up the stairs toward our bedroom. There at the top of the stairs was Bone! The area in which he was standing was dimly lit by a light from the television in our bedroom and by another one from the kitchen. Kurtis remembers seeing a vivid image of the cat, with his tail held characteristically high. Bone turned and looked straight at Kurtis, and then uttered the unique "mrr-mrr" sound, his peculiar trademark. Kurtis had just enough time to say, "Hello, Bone," before he vanished.

Kurtis has always been reluctant to talk about what he saw, but he did share some of his feelings:

"Bone looked as good as ever. I hesitate to talk about an experience like this. I feel it might detract from the meaning or significance of what I consider to be a spiritual event. I haven't been through much that compares to this happening, but seeing Bone certainly has had an influence on my view of the universe. I'm getting goose bumps just thinking about it!"

My husband and I feel very grateful that Bone came to visit us. I have always believed that animals have some sort of existence after death, and seeing Bone, and having my husband see him also, has only strengthened my convictions. Bone was buried in our new backyard as planned, and at his gravesite, we've planted a peach tree to memorialize his gorgeous "peachy" color.

Lance

...a most intelligent little feline who lived for 15 years in Maryland with Nancy Hartwell, a business executive who enjoys philology, writing, baking, and reading.

Lance was the smartest cat I have ever known. We were so close and communicated so much I often forgot she was a cat. From the time she was a kitten, she tried to talk to me, but it took me nearly nine months to figure out what she was saying. She would say "mee-uk" as soon as her milk dish was empty, and she would say "nooooooo" distinctly when she disagreed. As time went on, I began to figure out the meaning of the different sounds and meows she made. I believe she understood at least one hundred words or phrases, everything from "salmon" and "okay" to "tuna" and "let me fix it." She would become very annoyed if I did not understand her!

As my ability to understand her became more sophisticated, Lance began to shoot longer messages into my brain. I called her telepathic communications "b-mail," short for brain mail. One morning I went outside for a moment, and when I came back in, a strange message popped into my head. I heard, "That box made a noise." I knew perfectly well that I would *never* think in those words! Then I saw Lance looking at me as if to say, "Did you get my message?" and I realized she had told me that the phone had rung! I could hardly believe what was happening, but again and again, I received unusual messages that were unlike the way I would think or speak. One day while I was reading the paper, an ambulance went by the house with sirens screaming. I paid no attention to it, but Lance rushed over to the window to see the source of the noise, and then settled back beside me. She looked up and I heard her speak indignantly, "Humph! I have to do *everything* in this house!" Lance loved Mozart, but ran for her life whenever I played Wagner. Perhaps its strident passages rubbed her fur the wrong way! She would be angry after "The Ride of the Valkyrie," and complain lustily, "You and that darn box (CD player) did that to me again!" Once when I came back from the grocery store with my hands full of plastic bags, Lance tipped her head to one side and looked up at me fondly. Then I heard her say, "Sometimes you look really cute!" I laughed so hard I had to sit on the floor and give her a quick cuddle.

I was not the only person who could hear Lance. A very spiritual friend of mine, the leader of a secessionist party in Cameroon, lived in my apartment for about a year. After two days, he came to me and asked cautiously, "Does Lance talk?" When I said that she did, he responded, "Whew! I thought I was going crazy!" He never told me what she had said and I never asked. Another time, though, he had been designing a flag for his new country, and there were snippets of cloth all over the living room floor. He came to me and asked in disbelief, "Is it possible that Lance just told me to clean up my mess?"

"Not only is it possible. It is very probable!" I assured him.

Shaking his head, he went to get the vacuum. I heard him mumble, "This is the first time in my life that I am doing something because a cat told me to do it!"

He was even more shocked when Lance came back afterward to see if he had done a good job!

When I was reupholstering my couch, the "big chair," I turned it on its back so I could put on the skirt. Lance came upstairs to get me and took me downstairs to show me the couch. She seemed quite concerned. "Look what happened to the big chair." Then she added, "I didn't do it!" I tried to explain that it was okay and that I was just fixing it. She reacted by scolding me. "Okay? Fixing it? It's awful! Are you out of your mind? You can't even sit on it now." As she inspected the couch, the look on her face seemed to say, "I don't believe it. I just don't believe it!"

By now, you must be wondering why I called *her* "Lance," short for "Lancelot," an obviously masculine name. Well, I goofed! My daughter Becky and her friend picked Lance out of a Dumpster when she was about ten weeks old. She had been mistreated as well as abandoned, and she was scrawny and covered with fleas. Becky brought her home, where the kitty was so glad to be with us that she purred every time we looked at her! She was a gray tabby with an orange streak around her middle, and gold spots on her stomach. Neither my daughter nor I had any expertise in determining the sex of a cat. By the time we figured out our new cat was a female, it was too late to change her name because everyone was used to calling her "Lance." I kept meaning to ask her how she ended up in the Dumpster, but never got around to it.

Besides being smart, she was also the grouchiest cat I ever knew. My brother described her as being "fifty percent suspicious and fifty percent curmudgeonly." Lance was very possessive of me and was always *nasty* to my mother when she came to visit. My jealous cat would hide under the bedspread and lunge out to attack my mother, who had done absolutely nothing to provoke her. Lance also did not appreciate the four basketball players from the Central African Republic who were living in my basement for a while. We had only one bathroom, and it was on the second floor, where my bedroom and office were located. Lance considered my area to be her personal territory. She would plant herself on the stairway and not allow the men to come up! It was hilarious to see a man over six feet tall backing down because a cat would not let him pass. I would frequently have to intervene so the fellows could use the bathroom.

Lance was usually affectionate with me, but there were times that even I did not do things to suit her. One night I was not able to go to sleep, so quite uncharacteristically, I began to sing. Lance was on her corner of the bed and obviously did not approve of the serenade. Annoyed, she stood up and then flopped back down, as if to say, "Hey look. I'm trying to get some sleep!" I ignored her and launched into my second song. This time, she complained audibly, but I continued to ignore her. When I started a third melody, she marched over and bit me on the nose!

Another time, my Cameroonian friend was up all night in the bedroom next to mine, typing a petition for the United Nations. I usually left my bedroom door ajar so that Lance could come and go, but this time I got up to close the door because the typing was keeping me awake. Lance raced out ahead of me into the kitchen, where she thought I was going. I waited awhile for her to come back, but when she didn't, I went to bed without her. A few minutes later she scratched on the door, wanting to come in. I pretended not to hear her. Hey — it was three o'clock in the morning, and I was dead tired! She scratched more forcefully. I still ignored her.

Then she decided to pull out the big guns. She went to the dining room, got her ball with the bell in it, and began to hit the ball against the door. BLANG, blang, blang. BLANG, blang, blang. There was no way I could ignore that, so I let her in, closed the door, and we both went to sleep.

If I was sick or injured, Lance was extremely attentive. When I broke my leg, she pressed herself so tightly against me I thought our cells were going to be transposed. Another time I was really sick with the flu. The first day, Lance was very consoling. The second day, she was nice. The third day, she was fed up. She would still follow me around, but she let me know that enough was enough by behaving droopy and listless. I told her, "You don't have to be with me all the time."

She replied, "Yes, I do. It's my responsibility to take care of you, but this time you are being a royal pain."

When Lance was 14, she developed kidney disease. I had a real heart-to-heart talk with her as she neared death. "There is no need to be afraid," I reassured her. "You'll go to live with God. In a few years, we'll be together again."

I must have projected a mental image of God as a human being, because she immediately shot back, "For your information, you arrogant person, God is a CAT!"

Then I told her if she was in pain, I could take her to the vet and he would give her a shot. She seemed shocked. "Do you want to *kill* me?" she shrieked. Lance died at home in the afternoon, while I was at work.

Six weeks after her death, Lance came to visit me one night in the most extraordinary way. Our reunion began when she awakened me by walking on my stomach, something she had always done when she had something important to tell me. As I awoke, I saw the luminous form of Lance hovering above me! She was transparent and glowing magnificently with a light that reminded me of the aurora borealis. "You look so beautiful!" I told her. I reached up to hug her, but there was no substance, only air. What a strange sensation! I could see her, but I could not feel or touch her. Her image remained for a minute or so, and then faded away. Afterward I was overjoyed! It meant so much to me because our relationship had been so close, and I missed her terribly.

It has been more than 16 years since Lance died, but I still grieve for her. I wrote a letter to her not long ago. It explains my present situation, and gives a lot of insight into the way I still feel about her.

Dear Lance,

I'm the human for three wonderful cats now: Moondust, Samantha, and Topaz. They are cuddly and just as nice as they can be, but they don't talk to me the way you did. They don't complain when I forget to tell them that I've changed the sheets on the bed. They don't order my friends around, and they don't accuse me of being arrogant! They don't take one look at me when I come home and say, "Rough day, huh, Nance? Sit down over here and let me purr at you." I miss you, Lance, but I know you are safe in the arms of the Great Cat, and that one day, we'll be reunited.

                        Love always, Nancy

Nadine

...if you've never known a boy named Nadine, meet this one! He lived for nine years with Erika Moser, a customer service representative in Warwick, NY, who loves riding and gardening...and rescuing kittens.

Several years ago, my husband and I discovered a litter of three kittens who had been abandoned in a vacant lot across the street. The youngsters were about ten weeks old, and strangely enough, they all had abnormally short tails. Even though we had a house full of dogs and cats, everyone gladly accepted the newcomers, including our Pit Bulls, who slept with them every night!

Two of the kittens were black and one was all white, except for a black patch of hair between the ears. My husband examined the one with the black spot and proclaimed, "It's a girl!" We decided on the name "Nadine," after the character "Nadine" in the short-lived television series, *Twin Peaks*. It was a weird show, but a good one...just for fun. Television Nadine had a black patch over one eye to cover a bullet hole because her husband accidentally had shot her while they were on their honeymoon! We were so proud of the name we had chosen for our new kitty, so imagine our surprise a few days later when the vet told us that Nadine was a "he." Our naming of Nadine always reminded us of the Johnny Cash song about "A Boy Named Sue."

Nadine grew up to be more restless and independent than the other cats. If the weather was bad Nadine stayed indoors, but once conditions improved, he was always the first cat who wanted to go outside. Although he had been neutered, he would typically spend the night gallivanting around outdoors and then show up the next day when he was hungry.

By the time Nadine was nine, he had developed skin cancer on his ears. This wasn't surprising, since white cats are susceptible to this type of disease. To prevent it from spreading further, we had his ears cropped. About half of the height of each ear was removed in the surgery, and he had to wear a "daisy collar" around his neck so he couldn't scratch. With his shortened ears and his short tail, you could definitely pick him out in a crowd!

After his surgery, I brought my convalescing rascal into the house so that I could take care of him. Nadine had always been rather aloof, but now he changed and became affectionate and lovey-dovey. He loved sleeping on our bed, and unfortunately that big collar around his neck didn't leave much room for my husband and me. To make matters worse, he insisted on lying on my chest! I believe he knew that he had some serious problems and decided to stick around me for a while. But as soon as his ears healed two weeks later, Nadine became restless and wanted to go outside again. By then I had become very attached to him. I let him out reluctantly, expecting that he would return the next day as usual.

Days passed, and Nadine did not come home. I grew more and more worried. I called my neighbors to ask if they had seen him, and I looked everywhere, particularly in the woods around my house. For what seemed like hours, I stood on our deck and called him. A week passed...no Nadine. I was afraid I might never find him.

Then I had a dream that he had come home. It was an extraordinary dream, so vivid and real. The dream made such an impression on me that I told my husband I was eagerly looking forward to seeing Nadine again. I was sure I would see him that day, but he did not come home. I was so disappointed.

The following night I had another dream, just as realistic as the first. I saw Nadine playing in the backyard with my dog, Chesty, and my cat, Spice, both of whom had died years ago. I awoke believing that Nadine must surely be home now. All day I stood on my deck and repeatedly called for him. Again, I searched everywhere — but no Nadine.

The next day I continued to look for him, calling his name wherever I went. As evening approached, I stood on the deck wondering where to look next. It was very quiet. Suddenly, I heard a loud "meow." My heart skipped a beat. I knew it was Nadine! And I could tell exactly where the sound was coming from — a specific area underneath the deck. I called his name, but he didn't come out. Since the deck is quite low to the ground in many places, I thought he might be trapped under it and couldn't respond to my call. It was beginning to get dark, so I got a flashlight to look at the spot where I was certain I would see him. As I shone the light on the spot, I saw Nadine! I was elated! At last I had found him!

It was growing dark quickly, so I called a neighbor to help me. She held the flashlight while I crawled about 12 feet under the deck to retrieve Nadine. As I took hold of him, I was shocked. He was dead! I pulled his body out from under the wooden deck. He had obviously been dead for some time, as his body was very stiff. There was no sign of blood or injuries, so I don't know what caused his death. What I do know is that I heard a loud "meow," and 20 minutes later, I found my cat, Nadine, cold, rigid, and dead! Since rigor mortis had already developed, Nadine had to have died *hours* before I heard the "meow"!

As I look back, it is easier to put the extraordinary sequence of events together. In hindsight I understand so much more. Somehow Nadine knew I was looking for him. Three times he came to me in my dreams to let me know where he was. During my first dream, he came to tell me that he had come home. I suspect that he may have been injured and crawled under the deck to die. In the second dream, he let me know that he was in heaven and with some old family pets who had died several years before. The joy and playfulness Nadine showed me as he interacted with Chesty and Spice reassured me that he was happy in the afterlife. Since I still didn't understand his messages, Nadine came to me for a third time. He knew that I was worried and still looking for him. With a loud "meow," he showed me *where* to find his body. Then I understood! When I think about these events, I marvel at how this amazing cat communicated with me.

166

Puss E. Young

...an elegant black-and-white cat who was, for 13 years, the good friend of JoAnn M. Young, who loves gardening and reading. JoAnn lives in New Jersey.

Puss E. Young came to me as a sickly three-pound creature, sunburned, very thin, and nearly hairless. I didn't even know what type of animal he was, thinking perhaps he was a little squirrel that had fallen out of his nest. The vet was sure he was a kitten, but thought the baby would not survive because he was in such bad shape. He advised me to euthanize him. Thank God, I didn't listen! Instead, I took the little guy home and fed him baby food. I snuggled with him and let him "feel the love." Very gradually, he grew to be a gorgeous cat with long black-and-white hair, and weighed about 15 pounds.

For the first five years of his life, Puss was raised with my black-and-white Springer Spaniel called Shane, and they became fast pals. Since my dog became Puss's most treasured friend and companion, Puss grew up to behave more like a dog than a cat. He *hated* cats and *loved* dogs! Puss responded to barks, but never to meows. He even loved to roll onto his back and have his belly scratched, just like a dog. Every morning as I brushed my teeth, he would stand on the vanity and wait for me to fill the sink with water so he could have a drink. He also drank out of the toilet like a dog, even though he was in constant danger of falling in headfirst!

Puss was so special that everyone in the neighborhood knew and loved him. He was friendly to everyone and showed his affection by "hugging" people — wrapping his front legs around their neck and resting his head on their shoulder. In the summer, Puss liked to play and lie down in the field across the street. I had to whistle for him to come home because he would respond *only* to a whistle...like a dog! Puss would saunter down the path and then stop and wait until I came to pick him up. Then, true to his nature, Puss would wrap his front legs around my neck and hug me all the way home. How I loved that cat! What a precious relationship we enjoyed.

One snowy day in December, Puss was suddenly missing. He never strayed far from home, so I immediately put up posters and contacted shelters, but there was no response. Five days later, as I was driving home from work, I saw Puss. His body was on a street corner about five hundred feet from my house. Even though I had searched that area several times, his body had apparently been buried under the snow, which had now melted just enough to allow it to be visible. I stopped and ran to Puss, only to discover to my horror that a car had hit him and his face was missing! Despite the way I felt, somehow I managed to wrap up what was left of him in a blanket from my car and take him home. I laid his body on his favorite bench and woke my husband, who had been napping. While my husband dug a grave, I held Puss and talked to him until eventually I reluctantly placed him in the ground, said my goodbyes, and hurried into the house, as I couldn't bear to watch the burial.

The manner of Puss's death was painfully hard for me to accept. I felt intense grief, and believed that his death had been my fault. After all, I had been the one who let him go out in the snow. I wondered if he had suffered, and if he blamed me. With tears streaming down my face, I wished and prayed that I could pet Puss E. Young one more time.

Less than a day after the burial, I was lying on the couch thinking about Puss when suddenly, he was there! He was resting just above me on a pillow, facing away from me. He was close enough to touch. When I first saw him, I thought I was losing my mind. It wasn't a dream — I was wide-awake! I had no idea how it happened, but there he was. I remained motionless, afraid to move and not believing my eyes. After a few moments, I cautiously started to talk to him. "Hi, Puss," I said softly. "How are you? Hey, Puss, turn around. Come on, Puss. It's okay. Turn around and let me see your face." As I spoke, I noticed that his ears twitched, so I assumed he could hear me. Still, he didn't turn around. I continued talking to him for about a minute. Then, ever so slowly, I reached my hand up to pet him. I touched his hindquarters! It felt as if my hand were floating in a warm, soft, velvety material. It certainly didn't feel like fur. I had the strange sensation that my hand had gone slightly inside of him. It seemed to "sink" a little, but not to go through him.

Stroking him, I wondered why Puss didn't turn around. Perhaps he didn't want me to see his face, because it had been missing when I found him. I reassured Puss, "It's okay. I don't care what your face looks like. You can turn around." Still he wouldn't move. I sat up slowly and started to get off the couch to change my position. As I began to move, I lost sight of him briefly and then I heard a "meow." When I looked back, Puss was gone. I touched the pillow where he had been, and it felt warm.

After he was gone I felt quite calm, or perhaps a better word would be "serene." My serenity was accompanied by a profound sense of love. Truly, I had been blessed to have this experience. Several times after that, I saw Puss's shadow in the hallway outside my bedroom and sensed his presence. I am positive it was Puss because I heard the bell on his collar. Now when I hear his bell, I just smile and say "hi" to assure him I am all right. I honestly believe that Puss comes back from time to time to comfort me. His spirit feels my pain, my anguish, and my guilt. Returning is his way of thanking me for saving his life, and for giving him a wonderful home for 13 years. He comes to let me know that he misses me, too, but that he is doing fine.

I often think that the only meaningful foundation for a civilized world is human kindness and respect for all life. I recall one of my favorite stories, which illustrates this kindness and respect. Mr. Walsh was a photographer who was in Afghanistan helping to care for neglected animals in the zoo after it was bombed. Walsh still grieves for one animal he could not save — Marjan, the elderly lion who had lost his left eye in a grenade attack. Thanks to Mr. Walsh, the injured lion had medical attention and a warm den before he died in 2005, at the age of 25. Even though he could not save the lion, Walsh believes that the love and the care he gave the old fellow were worth the effort. "One day, we're all going to show up at the pearly gates, and St. Peter will be there," Walsh says. "But no one has ever seen St. Peter. How do we know he's not a blind old lion?"

Throughout the years, I have experienced profound love for several pets, but Puss was unique, and connected to me in a special way. A relationship equal to ours will never come again in my lifetime. Thank goodness, I will see him again. Puss is buried in one of his favorite spots in our yard. I planted a "pussy willow" tree there, with a little cat statue and flowers around it. Every night, I say good night to my friend, just as I did when he was alive. "Goodnight, Puss. See ya in the morning."

Muffin and *Queen Isis*

...Dorothy Hirst is a fascinating lady who writes that she is a spiritual medium. She lives in Grass Valley, California and enjoys taking care of feral cats. One of her cats, Muffin, was a lovely black stray who was her loving companion for just five years. Queen Isis was a mischievous Abyssinian cat who lived with Dorothy for seven years.

There are certain people who have the gift of extrasensory perception and are able to see and understand things the rest of us cannot, much as we might desire to do so. Dorothy Hirst is such a person. She realized early in her life that she had "inherited" this gift from her grandmother, who, like her, worked primarily with clairsentience and clairvoyance. Although Dorothy has never worked professionally as a medium, she has done many readings without charge for friends who requested them. Dorothy believes that early human beings had the gift of inner knowing, but now with the advance of civilization most people have lost it. Animals have also inherited the talent, which shows up when they return to us after they die or when they predict the future with surprising accuracy. Dorothy recalls years ago that her little dog Poncho began to howl for no apparent reason. She asked her father what was wrong with Poncho. He replied that perhaps a neighbor was ill and about to die, as dogs often howl prior to a death. The next day, it was Dorothy's *father* himself who fulfilled Poncho's "prophesy" when he died unexpectedly of a heart attack!

Dorothy feels the presence of deceased family members, friends, and pets, and then sees their image in her mind. The presence of these spirits is strong and undeniable. "In less than two years," said Dorothy, "I lost my husband, a son, and two cats, Muffin and Isis. They have all come to visit me." Dorothy also recalls seeing her Collie, "Lad," her Terrier mix, "Missy," and her Poodle mix, "Zoby." All three were together, and surprised Dorothy one day by walking into her living room. A few days later, her youngest son Larry, who was visiting her, looked up from reading his newspaper and exclaimed, "Oh, my gosh! Lad, Missy, and Zoby just walked in!" Dorothy realized then that the "gift" did not end with her.

Dorothy tells the stories of Muffin and Queen Isis, which continue to reveal her extraordinary powers:

Muffin was a beautiful black stray cat who befriended my husband and me when she was very young. She was our "tame feral" cat, and from the very beginning she came eagerly into our house, which is quite unusual for a cat who has never known human companionship, or what living inside was like. One of her favorite places was my husband's lap, where she snuggled and purred as if she had a little motor inside her. Although she liked being in the house with us, Muffin became quite insistent whenever she wanted to go outside. We would let her out, but she would always return to us quickly. It became her regular routine for nearly five years, until one day, Muffin didn't come back.

She was gone for more than a week, and I was increasingly concerned. I looked everywhere for her and was opening the front door constantly, calling her and hoping to see her coming home. After eight days, Muffin returned, but when I saw her, I felt sick and wept because it was obvious that she had been hit by a car. One hind leg was broken and the other was badly crushed. Her pelvic bone was broken as well. How she was able to drag her body to my front door, I will never know. She needed to go to the vet as quickly as possible, but first I gave her water and a bowl of food, both of which she gulped down. Afterward, I wrapped her in a big towel, and to my surprise she began to purr!

When I got to the vet, he told me that because her injuries were so severe and extensive, I should euthanize her. I felt very depressed. Six months earlier, I had lost my husband of 58 years, and now I was facing this tragic ordeal. I hated having to make the decision, but I reluctantly followed the vet's advice. Later, he commented, "This was the bravest cat I've ever seen!"

When I got home, I noticed the house felt so silent and so empty. Some days were more difficult than others. One especially hard day, I sat down to relax in the late afternoon. As I reached for a magazine on the coffee table, I was suddenly aware of something to one side of me. I looked up and saw my late husband sitting in a chair not too far from me. There was a patch of sunlight streaming through the patio door, a few feet from where he sat. Muffin was lying in his lap, purring, just as she used to do. I was overwhelmed with gratitude! My husband looked so well, and Muffin appeared beautiful, content, plump, and healthy. My husband looked at me as if to tell me not to grieve, because he had shown me that they were both fine. In just a few seconds, they were gone, and nothing remained but an empty chair and the patch of sunlight. "Oh, thank you," my heart breathed over and over again. "Thank you for showing me this!"

Queen Isis came to live with me when she was about four years old. Her owner had died, and the cat was taken to a store where she was made available for adoption. The first time I saw her, I immediately looked away, trying my best to ignore her. I did not intend to take her, and I knew that if I really looked at her, I wouldn't be able to resist. Avoiding her glance proved to be of no avail. She kept making noises to get my attention! Finally, I couldn't stand it any longer. I looked and took her home with me that day.

What a character this kitty turned out to be! She loved to dive under my throw rugs and then poke her head out. Queen Isis was appropriately named, with her willful, strong-minded, and sometimes downright

ornery attitude. She disliked all of my guests who visited *her* house — especially when they sat in *her* favorite chair. Isis would sit and stare at the intruding guest. If that did not make an impression, she would wrap her legs around the visitor's legs. Finally, her protest escalated to the point where she would move in with a few nips!

Isis displayed her naughtiness to me also, and I think her most obnoxious prank was the "Startle Game." Whenever I would lie down comfortably on my recliner and start to doze off, Isis would suddenly jump into my lap, landing firmly on me with all four feet, for no other reason than to wake me up! What an incorrigible tease she was, repeating those exasperating leaps. I can see her now, crouched in a stalking mode, watching and waiting for me to fall asleep. Once my breathing became soft and regular, that was her cue. Bam! She would leap onto me, delighting in my startled reaction.

Isis's health seemed fine, until one day she just stopped eating. No other symptoms were apparent, but the vet confirmed that she was quite ill with a liver disease, and her prognosis was poor. Because I could not get her to eat, I decided to euthanize her. Naturally, it was a tremendous shock to lose her so suddenly, and I agonized over whether or not I had made the right decision.

A few weeks later, in the middle of a quiet afternoon, I started to fall asleep on my recliner. Suddenly ... wham! I woke up with a start as I felt something jump into my lap. I believe it was Isis! She had come back to wake me up again with a jolt. It was odd that when I opened my eyes, there was nothing on my lap, but there is no doubt that I felt her weight as she leapt onto me. At first I was merely startled, but then I was tickled and smiled when I realized that even in the afterlife my little rascal is still a naughty tease! Perhaps she is saying, "So you thought you were rid of me? I'll show you!" So far she has jumped into my lap only once. Knowing her, however, I imagine she is planning another attack, anticipating just the right moment to execute the maximum startle!

"I am so grateful to be able to see spirits. It helps when grieving over the loss of loved ones. When I cross over, I expect many cats, dogs, and horses to welcome me. What a joy!"

...Dorothy Hirst

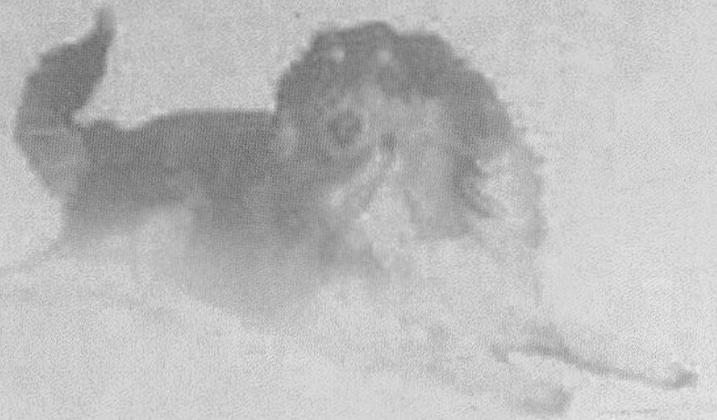

Animals in Heaven

There must be a heaven for the animal friends we love.

They are not human, yet they bring out

our own humanity . . . sometimes in ways

that other people cannot.

They do not worry about fame or fortune.

Instead, they bring our hearts

nearer to the joys of simple things.

Each day they teach us

little lessons in trust

and steadfast affection.

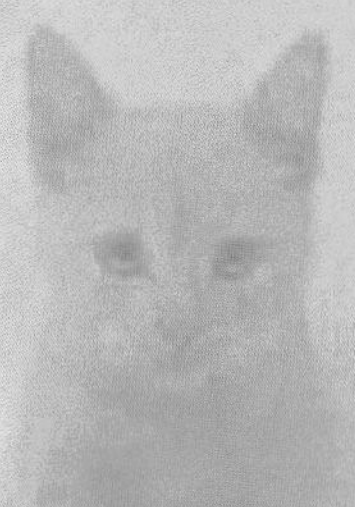

Whatever heaven may be,

there's surely a place in it, for friends as good as

these.

...author unknown

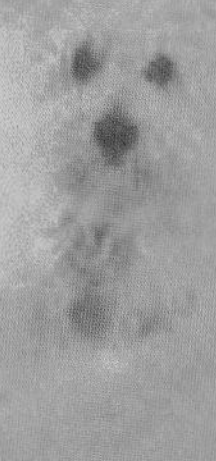

Printed in the United States
129185LV00004B